WINNING
THE HEART
OF GOD

WINNING THE HEART OF GOD

ROBB THOMPSON

ROYAL BOOKS

NASHVILLE

A Division of Thomas Nelson, Inc.
www.ThomasNelson.com

Published in Nashville, Tennessee by Thomas Nelson, Inc.

Editorial Consultant: Cynthia Hansen

Cover Design: Greg Lane

Library of Congress Cataloging-in-Publication Data

ISBN 0-7852-6487-6

Printed in the United States of America

02 03 04 05 06 PHX 5 4 3 2 1

Contents

Introduction   vii

Part 1: A Submitted Heart
David: A Man After God's Own Heart   3
The Subtle Trap of Rebellion   29
God's Way of Relating to Authority   55
Choose Obedience   93
God's Only Path to Fulfillment   105

Part 2: A Loyal Heart
The Foundation of Faithfulness   147
The Steadfast Loyalty of Our God   161
Loyalty: Our Link to Divinity   183
Loyalty Is a Choice   201

Notes   227
Acknowledgments   229
About the Author   230

INTRODUCTION

A vital element is missing from many Christians' lives—an element that is attained only by individual choice. It is the element of God's heart—of seeing everything pertaining to life on this earth the way God sees it.

It isn't that God doesn't want to impart His heart to His people; He emphatically does! But too often people are all caught up with their own selfish perspective. They are constantly thinking in terms of how things affect them: What can I get out of this situation? How can I maneuver my relationships so the people in my life become everything I want them to be?

Second Chronicles 16:9 (KJV) tells us that God actively searches for people with "perfect hearts": "For the eyes of the LORD run to and fro throughout the whole earth, to shew himself strong in the behalf of them whose heart is perfect toward him."

What does it mean to have a perfect heart toward God? The New International Version translates that phrase this way: ". . . whose hearts are fully committed to him." The New King James

Version says that God shows Himself strong "on behalf of those whose heart is loyal to Him." These are the people who win the heart of our faithful, covenant-keeping God because they have learned to respond to every situation from His perspective.

Over the years, my primary focus has been to help people develop a perfect heart toward God so they can become winners in every area of life. One thing I have not focused on is protecting my own interests. You see, I am convinced God will take care of me. I know He loves me. I know He is for me. Even if I were dropped off the Sears Tower, I might be as thin as a nickel when it was over, but somehow God would get me back on my feet!

These are not big faith statements for me. I don't sit up at night wringing my hands and wondering what is to become of me. I know I will be fine. I never spend time trying to understand why someone has wronged me. No matter what scandal erupts in front of me, I will not be changed because I have made a choice. My life isn't based on what any man thinks; it is based on what God thinks.

In this book, I want to answer the question, What does it take to win the heart of God? In order to do that, I'll show you the primary ingredients that must be present in your life to become a person "after God's own heart." You will find out that neither society nor a dictionary can define who you are and what your words mean. Only your heart gives definition to everything else in your life.

The most revealing attribute of spiritual immaturity is subjectivity—seeing things only from your perspective. So as you read this book, ask yourself this: Do I see situations only according to what is important to me and what I can get out of them? Or is God able to look at me and say, "This child of Mine is a person after My own heart"?

My prayer is that this book will help set you free so you can obtain "the missing element" for yourself. Allow the Holy Spirit to make the necessary adjustments in your life. Don't stop until your heart is perfect toward God. Only then will you be able to win His heart and enter into His perfect will for your life.

Part 1:

A Submitted Heart

Chapter 1

DAVID: A MAN AFTER
GOD'S OWN HEART

The prophet Samuel—a man on a divine mission—walked with purpose toward the small town of Bethlehem. Sadness filled his heart as he thought of Saul, the current king of Israel, who had just proven himself unworthy of the crown he wore. Now God had rejected Saul as king and sent Samuel to Bethlehem to the house of a man named Jesse. All Samuel knew was that once he arrived there, he would anoint one of Jesse's sons to be Israel's next king.

At Samuel's request, Jesse brought out his sons to pass before the prophet. All seven young men were tall, handsome, and impressive looking, yet Samuel chose none of them. As Jesse stood nearby, wondering what was happening, Samuel asked him, "Do you have any other sons?"

"Well, yes, there is one more son," Jesse admitted. "He is out in the fields tending sheep." To Jesse, his youngest son, David, seemed insignificant in comparison to his seven older sons. But Jesse was seeing the situation from man's perspective.

Young David finally arrived from the fields, having no idea what was going on. The Lord told the prophet Samuel, "This is the one!" Immediately Samuel took the horn of oil and anointed David in front of his brothers.

Why did Samuel pass over the seven older brothers? Because of what God told the prophet as he gazed with approval at Eliab, Jesse's strapping firstborn son: "Do not look at his appearance or at his physical stature, because I have refused him. For the LORD does not see as man sees; for man looks at the outward appearance, but the LORD looks at the heart" (1 Sam. 16:7).

This, then, is the key. God doesn't look at the outside of man; He looks at the heart.

People wonder all the time why they seem stuck in life, never getting beyond mediocrity and chronic defeat. But these people don't have a problem with the external circumstances of their lives. They don't even have a problem with sin. The problem lies in their hearts.

"A MAN AFTER MY OWN HEART"

From the moment Samuel anointed David, the young man began a lifelong love affair with God, and God began to move mightily in David's life.

Second Corinthians 8:1 uses a phrase that applies here: "Moreover, brethren, we make known to you the grace of God bestowed on the churches of Macedonia." The "grace of God bestowed" is exactly what happened on the day Samuel anointed David. God's grace was bestowed on David to become like Him.

From that moment on, David's life would be defined by his constant pursuit of the Lord and his deep yearning to please God in everything that he was.

A study of David's life reveals that he chose to make the pursuit of God his life's ambition. Later God would call David "a man after My own heart" (Acts 13:22).

In the entire Bible, God referred to only two men with such affection. First, Matthew 3:13–17 relates the time Jesus came to John the Baptist on the shores of the Jordan River. John recognized Jesus as the Son of God and exclaimed, "I need to be baptized by You, and You are coming to me?" But Jesus told John, "Permit it to be so now, for thus it is fitting for us to fulfill all righteousness."

So John obeyed, baptizing Jesus in the river. As Jesus rose out of the water, the Spirit of God descended from heaven like a dove and rested upon Him. Then God spoke out of heaven: "This is My beloved Son, in whom I am well pleased."

The only other man spoken about with such affection in all the Bible was David. According to God's assessment, David was a man after His own heart.

But what does it mean to be a person after God's heart? Well, the meaning of the word *after* in the original Greek is interesting. We might think it means to come behind something that has gone before. But actually the word after means to resemble; to follow; to be in pursuit of; to be right up next to; to aspire; and to desire to be like.

David was a man after God's heart because he aspired to be like God. David wanted everything about his life to reflect God.

David wanted to look like Him, think like Him, talk like Him, and act like Him. He wanted to be everything God ever wanted him to be. And because of David's intense desire to be like the Most High, God was able to use him in a mighty way.

WHY SAUL WAS REJECTED

Even as a young man, David made the choice to follow after God. He might have seemed like an insignificant son of a man who had many sons. However, because of David's choice, he became God's choice for king.

But what had caused God to reject King Saul in the first place? First Samuel tells us that Saul rejected God before God rejected him as king.

Several years earlier, the children of Israel had asked for a king because they wanted to be like all the nations surrounding them. God chose Saul to be that man. At the time, Saul was a humble man who really loved God. In his early years as king, Saul often led Israel to victory over their enemies.

But things changed for Saul as the years passed by. Pride crept into his soul, and he began to think that he could do no wrong.

Then King Saul made a grave error at Israel's battle with the Amalekites. God had instructed Saul, "Now go and smite Amalek, and utterly destroy all that they have, and spare them not; but slay both man and woman, infant and suckling, ox and sheep, camel and ass" (1 Sam. 15:3 KJV).

Saul didn't follow those divine instructions, however. Verse 9

(KJV) tells us what Saul did instead of killing all the Amalekite people and livestock as God had commanded:

> Saul and the people spared Agag, and the best of the sheep, and of the oxen, and of the fatlings, and the lambs, and all that was good, and would not utterly destroy them: but every thing that was vile and refuse, that they destroyed utterly.

Suddenly the word of the Lord came to Samuel in the night, saying, "I greatly regret that I have set up Saul as king, for he has turned back from following Me, and has not performed My commandments" (v. 11).

Samuel went to Saul, and Saul said to him, "Blessed be thou of the LORD: I have performed the commandment of the LORD" (1 Sam. 15:13 KJV).

All over the world, there are Christians who absolutely believe they are doing exactly what God told them to do, even though they are not doing what is written. Therefore, the only way they can believe that they are obeying God's instructions is to live outside the parameters of God's Word.

That was King Saul's fatal mistake, and Samuel confronted him with it. The prophet asked Saul, "If you followed God's instructions so precisely, what is this bleating of sheep and lowing of oxen that I hear?"

"Oh, that?" Saul said. "We're going to have a big sacrifice before the Lord! We're going to perform our religious duty of worship before God because He has given us a great victory!"

Samuel wasn't fooled. He said, "Be quiet, Saul! You have not obeyed the voice of the Lord. Because you have rejected the word of the Lord, God has rejected you as king over Israel."

At first, Saul tried to make excuses for himself. But finally he admitted, "I have sinned against God."

When people get caught in their wrongdoing, they often want to do whatever they need to do to get out of their uncomfortable situation. But seldom do they want to change from the inside out. Too many people live this type of "outside Christianity" every day of their lives; meanwhile, their hearts remain unchanged before God.

Even after Saul was told that the Lord had rejected him as king, Saul's big concern was that Samuel would give him an external show of support by offering a sacrifice with him before the people.

From that time on, Saul was king of Israel in name, but not in heart, for God had already chosen his successor—a young man after His own heart.

A SOLID FOUNDATION

Here is something you have to understand in your pursuit to win God's heart: every demonic attack that invades your life is aimed at destroying your foundation. The storms of life that infringe on your peace, cause discomfort or disillusionment, or steal your ability to live a life filled with God's presence and power are designed to challenge the very truths upon which you have built your life.

That's why Jesus warned us to be careful how we build our foundation:

But why do you call Me "Lord, Lord," and do not do the things which I say? Whoever comes to Me, and hears My sayings and does them, I will show you whom he is like: He is like a man building a house, who dug deep and laid the foundation on the rock. And when the flood arose, the stream beat vehemently against that house, and could not shake it, for it was founded on the rock. But he who heard and did nothing is like a man who built a house on the earth without a foundation, against which the stream beat vehemently; and immediately it fell. And the ruin of that house was great. (Luke 6:46–49)

David was a man whose spiritual foundation remained intact, no matter how many storms beat upon it. David faced many hardships and adversities in his life, but that strong foundation was never shaken. No matter what happened to him, David never moved.

SEEING THE GIANT
FROM GOD'S PERSPECTIVE

An interesting characteristic is shared by those who choose to pursue God as David did. Wherever these believers go, the presence of God that they carry with them causes what is wrong in others' lives to be revealed. At times they can make people angry just being in the same room! Meanwhile, these believers who have been branded by the Holy Spirit in their hearts stand there in innocence with absolutely no idea why people are upset with them. This very same thing happened to Stephen in Acts 7 when the mob recognized the Spirit of God upon him and then ran at him and stoned him to death.

These believers are not people who fit in and get along with the crowd. They have an entirely different thought pattern from that of the crowd. Why are they so different from others? Because they think from a divine perspective rather than from a human perspective.

This characteristic was certainly evident in David's life. For instance, not long after Samuel had anointed the young man, Israel went to war against the Philistines. Jesse told David to take food to his older brothers, who were stationed out on the battlefield with the rest of the Israelite army.

While David was there, the Philistine giant named Goliath came out in front of all the Israelite soldiers to taunt them. The huge man, who stood about nine feet six inches tall, was armed to the teeth. First Samuel 17:5–7 describes Goliath's enormous pieces of armor:

> He had a bronze helmet on his head, and he was armed with a coat of mail, and the weight of the coat was five thousand shekels of bronze. And he had bronze armor on his legs and a bronze javelin between his shoulders. Now the staff of his spear was like a weaver's beam, and his iron spearhead weighed six hundred shekels; and a shield-bearer went before him.

Goliath walked back and forth, yelling insults at Israel and challenging anyone who might dare fight him to come. But all the mighty warriors of Israel stood back and trembled. Every time Goliath stood up and blared out his insults, the men became only more afraid.

But David's reaction was completely opposite from theirs. He might have been just a teenager who was five feet six inches tall with red hair and a ruddy complexion, yet he had a strong foundation of faith in the God of Israel.

David arrived at the battlefield in time to hear one of Goliath's insulting outbursts against God and the army of Israel. After delivering the food, David asked some of the men, "What is going on with this character named Goliath?"

Immediately David's oldest brother, Eliab, turned on him. "I know your heart, little brother," Eliab said. "I know your wicked pride. I know your evil thoughts."

You see, a person who is after God's heart is always under scrutiny because he cannot be understood. That person may respond to a situation in a way that people consider strange, but somehow it usually turns out to be the right way. That was true throughout David's life.

So David decided he would fight the giant. The young man went to King Saul's tent and told the king he accepted the challenge. He explained that he had been practicing as a shepherd, killing both a lion and a bear while protecting his sheep.

At first Saul wouldn't hear of sending such a small youth against the Philistine giant, who was trained as a man of war from his youth. Then he said that David should at least wear the king's armor so he would look more like a warrior. David told the king, "Thanks, but no thanks." You see, David wasn't going out there to fight Goliath; he was going out there to shut the giant's mouth!

David wasn't thinking, *When I fight this guy, I'm going to beat him!* He was thinking, *No one talks that way about God and gets away with it!* A man who is after God's heart doesn't primarily think about what he is going to get out of anything. He thinks about what he can give. David was accepting his responsibility to uphold the honor of his God and his people.

David went down to a nearby stream, found five smooth stones, and put them in his pouch; then he boldly went out to meet the giant. As Goliath mocked and cursed the young man, David grabbed one of those smooth stones, put it in his sling, and started running toward the giant, swinging his sling. Goliath just rolled his head back and laughed in derision at David— revealing an open spot on his forehead that made the perfect target. David sent the rock flying, sinking it into Goliath's brain and causing the giant to fall headlong to the ground.

Once Goliath hit the deck, everyone in the Israelite army quickly became brave and started running after all the Philistines. In no time at all, the enemy was routed. David ran over to Goliath and picked up the huge sword that the giant had intended to use to destroy him. Then David cut off the giant's head with it and took that huge head back to Saul on a platter! "Here is your enemy's head, your majesty. I am delivering it to you!" The bold faith of one young man vindicated the honor of God and Israel! If the truth were ever revealed, we would quickly discover that this is a picture of our struggle with Satan and his assistants—only the roles are reversed. We are the giants, his thoughts are the stones. As we laugh at him, he hurls a thought at us that momentarily knocks us down. While we are complaining of the injustice of the present situation, he comes over to us taking the mighty sword of authority and the spirit to quickly cut off our life from God. It's then that God's delivering power cannot get to us.

DAVID BEHAVED WISELY
BEFORE GOD AND THE KING

Earlier David had spent time in Saul's court, playing his harp before the king. You see, ever since Saul had rejected the word of the Lord, he had been plagued at times by an evil spirit. David's music seemed to soothe the king and cause the evil spirit to depart. After David's victory over the Philistine giant, the king insisted that he remain at the royal court, and he appointed David as captain over a thousand men. As time went by, however, it became more and more apparent to Saul that the Spirit of the Lord had departed from him and now rested upon David.

David always behaved wisely in front of the people. He never made a mistake. He never broke rank. He kept his heart right. He never rebelled against Saul. He never said anything concerning the king except that Saul was the Lord's anointed, even though David knew that he himself had already been anointed king as far as God was concerned.

The young man understood an important spiritual principle: if you know that God has called you to do something, don't act on that knowledge by trying to make it come to pass on your own. God does all the acting that ever needs to be done. You never have to do one thing. Let me clarify this. From the time you believe that God has instructed you to occupy a position or be released from the one you are presently in, you must from this time on never act on your own behalf. God only allows you to react to another's actions against you. David reacted to Saul's attempts to kill him by running away, avoiding Saul as well as staying out of his demonically driven path. David would never rebel against God's anointed. An example of this is when Saul was sleeping in a cave and David cut away a piece of Saul's robe. The Bible tells us that David's heart smote him. The moment you act according to your natural efforts is the moment you have lost what God wants you to have.

Saul's jealousy of David increased as David's favor grew with the people. One day as David was playing his harp before the king, Saul threw his spear at him, barely missing him. Saul tried to kill David twice that same day, but David avoided Saul's presence for a while and refused to say anything against the king.

The day came when David had to leave Saul's court or be killed. This is where we see David's response to Saul's backslidden humanity. For years, Saul's jealousy drove him to try hunting David down to kill him, forcing David to stay on the run with the men who had gathered around him.

On one such hunt, Saul retired into a cave to relieve himself. Unbeknownst to Saul, David and his men were hiding deeper in that same cave.

David's men said to him, "Your enemy is now in your hands!"

But instead of ordering Saul's death, David crept over unseen to Saul and secretly cut off a piece of his robe.

Yet even though David had shown mercy to Saul—even though Saul was the one pursuing him—the Bible says that David's heart smote him because he had touched the Lord's anointed (1 Sam. 24:5–6). He cried out, "Oh, God, forgive me! I never should have touched Your anointed."

No matter how unjustly King Saul treated David, he never sinned in his heart against the king. In fact, during the years Saul hunted David, David called Saul many things: his father, a champion, the anointed of the Lord, and the one blessed by God. But whenever David said anything about Saul, it was always what God had already said about him.

Years later, Saul's pursuit of David finally ended when Saul and his three sons were killed in a battle with the Philistines. David didn't rejoice when Saul was killed. He didn't say, "He got what he deserved!" On the contrary, David mourned the deaths of Saul and his son Jonathan—David's covenant friend. David even sang a song to honor them that began, "The beauty of Israel is slain upon thy high places: how are the mighty fallen!" (2 Sam. 1:19 KJV).

A BROKEN AND CONTRITE HEART

David then went to Hebron and waited there until he knew whether the people wanted him to be king. It was there that the men of Judah came to anoint David as their new king. Once again, David didn't try to make anything come to pass on his own; he kept his heart right as he waited for God to bring His plan for him to pass.

By the time King David was fifty years old, he had won victory after victory over the surrounding kingdoms and was greatly loved by his people. But the man who was after God's own heart wasn't perfect. A time came when he made a serious error in judgment and committed a grave sin for which he would suffer consequences the rest of his life.

Choosing to stay home from the battlefield at a time "when kings go forth to battle" (2 Sam. 11:1 KJV), David allowed himself to lust after and then commit adultery with a woman named Bathsheba. For nine months, David was out of fellowship with God. He even issued an order to have Bathsheba's husband, Uriah the Hittite, killed.

But then Nathan the prophet confronted King David with his sin, saying, "You are the man!" (2 Sam. 12:7). David's response to Nathan's words gives us another indication of why God called him a man after His own heart. He immediately repented with a broken and contrite heart.

David wrote his response of contrition and repentance in Psalm 51:

> Have mercy upon me, O God,
> According to Your lovingkindness;
> According to the multitude of Your tender mercies,
> Blot out my transgressions.
> Wash me thoroughly from my iniquity,
> And cleanse me from my sin.

> For I acknowledge my transgressions,
> And my sin is always before me. (vv. 1–3)

The next verse is a statement from David's heart. This same heart understanding must be planted deep inside you if you are to walk closely with God.

> Against You, You only, have I sinned,
> And done this evil in Your sight—
> That You may be found just when You speak,
> And blameless when You judge. (Ps. 51:4)

You see, every sin that is ever committed is ultimately against God. Jesus said it like this: "Inasmuch as you did it to one of the least of these My brethren, you did it to Me" (Matt. 25:40).

Every sin you commit is a sin against God. When you rebel, you rebel against Him. Every bad attitude, every act of disobedience, every stepping out of line, every instance of "doing things your own way" is a revolt against God Himself. And with every revolt, you reenact the scene at the Garden all over again.

For instance, you may have lashed out at your boss, your spouse, or your children, but that sin is not against them; it was just directed toward them. You have actually sinned against God: "Against You, You only, have I sinned." Of course, other people always pay the price for your sin. Uriah paid the price for David's adultery with his life, as did the child who was born to Bathsheba as a result of her union with David.

David mourned over his sin as a man of heart. But he didn't

mourn for himself; he mourned over Bathsheba's suffering. He knew that he was the one at fault, and he wanted to comfort her: "Lord, don't let her come out of this empty-handed because of what I have done. I'm to blame for this, not her." God granted David's plea for mercy and granted him another child by Bathsheba—a son named Solomon.

After writing Psalm 51, his psalm of forgiveness, it is historically believed that David wrote Psalm 32:

> Blessed is he whose transgression is forgiven,
> Whose sin is covered.
> Blessed is the man to whom the LORD does not impute
> iniquity [does not lay sin to his charge],
> And in whose spirit there is no deceit. (vv. 1–2)

David knew he was forgiven for his sin, and he accepted that forgiveness. You see, a man of heart doesn't carry around the burden of guilt. He always makes sure he gets things straightened out with God; but once he has done that, he is finished with it. It is over.

Later David made another big mistake when he ordered a census to be taken of his people, contrary to God's instructions (2 Sam. 24:1–17). God then told him to choose the consequence of his sin: seven years of famine, three months in the hand of an enemy, or three days of pestilence. David prayed, "Lord, I know You. You are merciful. I choose three days in Your hands."

Pestilence spread throughout all of Israel for three days, and thousands died from the plague. David cried out for mercy for the people, saying, "Surely I have sinned, and I have done wickedly; but these sheep, what have they done? Let Your hand, I pray, be against me and against my father's house" (v. 17). Again, this cry reveals the heart of David. As Philippians 2:4 notes, David looked out "not only for his own interests, but also for the interests of others."

MORE CONSEQUENCES OF SIN— REBELLION IN THE CAMP

David had been forgiven for his sin, but some consequences lingered for the rest of his life. When he was about sixty years old, something terrible happened with his beloved son Absalom. Absalom was the best-looking man in the entire country with a long mane of flowing black hair. It was said of Absalom that he got a haircut once a year and that the haircut yielded two hundred shekels (three pounds) of hair (2 Sam. 14:26)! Everyone loved Absalom. People looked up to him, and his father, David, was very proud of him.

But Absalom killed his half brother Amnon in a misguided attempt to protect the honor of his sister (2 Sam. 13:1–29). Murder hadn't left David's household. Absalom ran away out of fear of David's retribution. Three years later, David summoned him to return home. However, Absalom was still forbidden to come into his father's presence.

So Absalom returned to Jerusalem with bitterness in his heart and secret plans to take over the throne. Two years later, he decided to use Joab as his way back into his father's presence.

When Joab didn't respond to his summons, Absalom first burned Joab's field of barley and then told him, "Now you will listen to me! I want to talk to my father!" Joab relayed the message, and David received the son he loved so much into his presence once again.

Absalom really didn't want to see his father; he just wanted to be restored to the king's favor so he could execute his devious plan to usurp the throne. Absalom began going to the city gates each day to talk to the people who traveled in and out to see the king, who was the judge and arbitrator of everyone's disputes and lawsuits. Since every dispute has a winner and a loser, Absalom would find the loser and say, "Hey, friend, how did it go today?"

The loser of the dispute would say dejectedly, "Not so well, Absalom. The king just didn't see things my way."

Then the person would bow his knee in obeisance to Absalom, but the wily prince would pick him up and say, "You don't need to bow your knee to me. Look, you should have won your case. If only I were the judge, then justice could come to the land!"

In that way, Absalom began to gather people to himself. Soon he had enough people to try to overthrow his father's throne.

What was the man who was after God's own heart going to do in the situation? What was he going to say? How was he going to act? At that particular point in his life, David had a choice: (1) he could choose his flesh and try to kill this person who posed a threat to his rule—in other words, become exactly like Saul; or (2) he could remain the man of heart he had always been.

David chose the latter course of action. He decided to depart from Jerusalem with his household, his servants, and his closest supporters. As David and his company left the city, a man named Shimei, a member of the house of Saul, saw the king and yelled, "You are finally getting what you deserve for what you did to Saul! You're about to run into some rough stuff. It's over, King David. You're history!" Shimei even picked up stones and threw them at David (2 Sam. 16:5–13).

David's guards asked, "You are the king! Are you going to let him do this to you?"

David said, "Leave him alone. Let him say what he will. If my son has turned against me, how much more should this Benjamite do so?"

Shimei continued to curse and throw stones at the king, but the man after God's own heart walked on. Finally Shimei left.

To David, it must have seemed that most of Israel was siding with Absalom. Absalom took David's concubines who had been left behind to take care of the palace; he took David's closest advisor, a man named Ahithophel.

David sat down and wrote Psalm 3:

> LORD, how they have increased who trouble me!
> Many are they who rise up against me.
> Many are they who say of me,
> "There is no help for him in God." (vv. 1–2)

People were telling David, "You see, God is paying you back. You are getting what you have coming to you. God is the One making your life miserable. He is on your case. He is against you. That means there is no help for you, David. God can't even put out His arm and save you anymore because you've gone too far this time."

I hear this kind of talk from people all the time. They think God has something to do with their failures in life. Pay close attention to David's response to all the words of doubt and accusation that had been hurled at him: "But You, O LORD, are a shield for me, my glory and the One who lifts up my head" (Ps. 3:3). When everything looked hopeless, this man of heart knew he had to turn to his God for comfort and encouragement.

Psalm 38 is another of David's psalms reflecting his intimate thoughts during this painful time:

> I am feeble and severely broken;
> I groan because of the turmoil of my heart.
> Lord, all my desire is before You;
> And my sighing is not hidden from You.
> My heart pants, my strength fails me;
> As for the light of my eyes, it also has gone from me.
> My loved ones and my friends stand aloof from my plague,
> And my relatives stand afar off.
> Those also who seek my life lay snares for me;
> Those who seek my hurt speak of destruction,
> And plan deception all the day long.
> But I, like a deaf man, do not hear;
> And I am like a mute who does not open his mouth.
> Thus I am like a man who does not hear,
> And in whose mouth is no response.
> For in You, O LORD, I hope;
> You will hear, O Lord my God. (vv. 8–15)

Something happened inside this man of heart when his friends turned on him. It was bad enough that his number one son—the one upon whom the sun rose and fell—decided to take over his kingdom. Then everyone was calling him weak because he was running from his son. And if that wasn't bad enough, his closest counselor—one of his best friends—chose to defect to the opposing side!

David talked further of his pain in Psalm 55:

> For it is not an enemy who reproaches me;
> Then I could bear it.
> Nor is it one who hates me who has exalted himself
>   against me;
> Then I could hide from him.
> But it was you, a man my equal,
> My companion and my acquaintance.
> We took sweet counsel together,
> And walked to the house of God in the throng. (vv. 12–14)

Then starting in verse 16, David once again turned to God for his help:

> As for me, I will call upon God,
> And the LORD shall save me.
> Evening and morning and at noon
> I will pray, and cry aloud,
> And He shall hear my voice.
> He has redeemed my soul in peace
>   from the battle that was against me,

For there were many against me.

God will hear, and afflict them,

Even He who abides from of old. Selah

Because they do not change,

Therefore they do not fear God.

He has put forth his hands against those

who were at peace with him;

He has broken his covenant.

The words of his mouth were

smoother than butter,

But war was in his heart;

His words were softer than oil,

Yet they were drawn swords.

Cast your burden on the LORD,

And He shall sustain you;

He shall never permit the righteous

to be moved [made to fall, to slip, or to fail]. (vv. 16–22)

All these psalms demonstrate that David understood well his covenant relationship with God.

THE ATTRIBUTES OF A MAN
AFTER GOD'S HEART

David showed himself to be a man who walked in covenant love when he took care of Jonathan's son Mephibosheth. After the death of Jonathan, Mephibosheth was afraid that David was going to destroy him. But David said concerning Jonathan's son,

DAVID: A MAN AFTER GOD'S OWN HEART

"He will eat at my table the rest of his life. Give him back all the land that was ever taken from Saul's family, and the family of Saul's servant Ziba will work the land for him so all his descendants may be able to enjoy it" (2 Sam. 9:6–11).

Throughout his life, David showed himself to be a man of love. He thought of other people before himself, and even though he wasn't perfect, he always tried to do what was right. For instance, one time three of his mighty men risked their lives to get him something he had voiced a longing for—water from the well of Bethlehem. But David asked, "How can I drink a cup of water that my men risked their lives to get for me?" Then he poured out the water as an offering to the Lord (2 Sam. 23:15–17).

David was a forgiver, for no matter how many wrongs King Saul committed against him, David always forgave him. Many years later, David also forgave his son Absalom for what he had done. David even cried for Absalom when his son was killed as a consequence of his rebellion. We must realize that anything God has created he created for the giver of it. When David forgave Absalom, Absalom did not benefit from the forgiveness because his rebellion ultimately destroyed him. David was the one who avoided the consequences of unforgiveness.

David was also a man of intense fairness and integrity. He sought to uphold the honor of the king who continually tried to kill him. For instance, after Saul's death, a man came to David and said he had killed Saul, expecting a reward. David replied, "You thrust through the anointed of the Lord, and now you shall be thrust through!" (See 2 Sam. 1:2–16.) David's attitude toward

Saul never changed; he would not touch God's anointed and he would not tolerate anyone who did.

David was a man of submission. He always gave himself to the will of those whom God had placed as authorities over him (whether it was his father, Jesse; King Saul; the prophet Nathan; or God Himself). Let's define submission. First, let us break up the word. *Sub Mission,* a secondary mission. For practical purposes submission is "the willingness to bow my knee before men in order to satisfy the requirements of Heaven."

Finally, at the end of his life, David was a giver. He sought the Lord for permission to build a house for God. When God replied with a negative answer, David did not flinch. He smiled back at God and said, "God you may have told me that I could not build you a house, but you never told me I couldn't pay for it." He went on to say, "But, God, who am I and who are my people that we should be able to offer so willingly as this? All we have, You have given to us. Everything I have, You have given to me" (1 Chron. 29:10–19).

Truly David was a man after God's own heart, and he lived his life from his heart. No matter what happened to him, nothing was going to deter him from being who God had called him to be.

Now the question is this: What is the condition of your heart? When this life on earth is over, will it be said of you that you always lived life from your own perspective—that you were a person who pursued your own desires more than you pursued God? Or will it be said concerning you that God bent down and whispered, "I have found in you the one I am searching for, a person who is after My own heart"?

My friend, the entire Bible revolves around that one word—heart. That is the place from which you are to live your life. That is the only place from which you can build a sure foundation for your life. You can win the Father's heart only when you love Him as David did—from the depths of your heart with everything that you are.

So let's explore further what David understood so well: how to become a person of heart, continually following after God's heart as you walk through this life.

• *Chapter 2* •

THE SUBTLE TRAP
OF REBELLION

S aul had everything going for him. He stood head and shoulders taller than anyone else in Israel. When the children of Israel cried out for a king, Saul was God's first choice. And in his first few years as the king of Israel, Saul and his army prevailed in their battles with the surrounding enemy nations.

But as we have seen, a fatal flaw showed up in Saul's character during Israel's battle with the Amalekites. God had told Saul to utterly wipe out the Amalekite people because of their great sin against His people. "Go after them, Saul," the Lord commanded. "Kill everything—men, women, children, and livestock. Burn down their cities. I want their name wiped off the face of the earth."

However, Saul decided to follow his own idea of obedience to God in the battle against the Amalekites. After all, he reasoned, why kill all those valuable livestock? What harm would there be in saving the best of the animals to offer as an impressive sacrifice to the Lord before the people? So Saul had the Amalekites killed but left the king alive, as well as the best of the healthy sheep and oxen. Saul had fallen victim to the deceptive trap of rebellion.

Afterward, the Lord awakened Samuel in the night and informed him, "I am sorry I ever made Saul king. He has turned back on My commandments." The king who once had everything going for him had just lost it all through rebellion. God was unimpressed that Saul planned on offering the animals he had spared to the Lord as a burnt sacrifice. As Samuel told Saul, "To obey is better than sacrifice" (1 Sam. 15:22).

REBELLION IS WITCHCRAFT

God takes rebellion very seriously. Read carefully what Samuel said about it as he and Saul stood in the midst of the bleating and lowing of Amalekite livestock: "For rebellion is as the sin of witchcraft, and stubbornness is as iniquity and idolatry" (1 Sam. 15:23).

Obedience is better than sacrifice, and rebellion is as the sin of witchcraft. But if you study the original Hebrew of verse 23, you will find that the translators added "as the." The original text simply says that rebellion is witchcraft.

Why is rebellion the same as witchcraft? Because the source of both is control. Rebellious people don't want to give control to the authority that God has placed over them; they want to control the situation.

Instead of maintaining a clean conscience upward with the divine authority over him, Saul turned downward for advice and let the people below him pollute his mind with rebellion. Then he tried to blame the people for his sin, telling Samuel, "The people took of the plunder, sheep and oxen, the best of the things which should have been utterly destroyed, to sacrifice to the LORD your God in Gilgal" (1 Sam. 15:21).

You can learn from Saul's costly mistake. People who are above you in authority are not the ones who pollute your mind with rebellion; the people who are below you do that. People above you are usually encouraging you, saying, "Come on, you can do it! You can win!" Those who are behind you or even those who are equal to you are the ones who may try to poison your mind and build a case for rebellion. But remember, rebellion is witchcraft. You need to do everything possible to make sure you stay out of it!

Some may ask, "What was so bad about Saul keeping a few sheep and oxen in order to sacrifice them in worship to God? How could God blame him for that? He just made a mistake. What's the big deal?"

God explained what the big deal was in Saul's actions that day. The Lord told Saul, "I am rejecting you as king because you rejected the word of the Lord—because you deliberately disobeyed what I told you to do, and obedience is better than sacrifice." God could no longer trust Saul because Saul had begun to make his own decisions.

In recent years, archaeologists have uncovered bones from animals in the region where the Amalekites lived. Some of those bones showed traces of syphilis! Perhaps the reason God wanted all those animals destroyed was that they were diseased. Saul didn't know the reason, but he didn't have to know the reason in order to obey God. It was none of Saul's business why God told him to destroy all the Amalekites' livestock. God's instructions weren't open for discussion.

Let us remember that God doesn't need to explain Himself; He just needs to be obeyed.

Now, you may think I'm too hard when it comes to this rebellion issue. But do you realize how many honors and blessings you have passed up in your life because of rebellion? Do you realize how many things God wanted to do for you but couldn't because you thought you knew better?

In Saul's case, pride and disobedience gave birth to rebellion, and in the end he lost the kingdom God had given him to rule. Pride and disobedience will give birth to rebellion in your life as well. (It may not cost you a kingdom, but I can guarantee you this, my friend: if you only knew what rebellion has already cost you, you'd do everything possible to eliminate it from your life!)

SATAN'S INSIDIOUS INFLUENCE
ON MODERN-DAY SOCIETY

We've seen the high price Saul paid for his rebellion. But just what is rebellion?

Rebellion refers to a person's attempt to take authority in an area over which God has not given him the authority. A rebellious person resists and refuses to submit to his proper authority, casting off the allegiance God has required of him.

Sadly, rebellion has swept through today's society at every level.

The influence of Satan's kingdom in this world is so pervasive that even the Church has succumbed to the power of self.

Whether you realize it or not, the people you know and the things you experience every day are continually being influenced by things other than the Lord Jesus Christ. Through every form of media available to man today, modern society teaches people that:

- Indulgence in lustful pleasures is the norm, and abstinence is abnormal.

- Right is wrong and wrong is right.

- If it feels good, do it—whatever "it" is.

- You only need to show kindness to those who deserve it. Don't waste love on people who have done nothing to benefit you.

- You have the right to get back at people who have hurt you. Turning the other cheek is for cowards.

- Taking care of number one is the main priority.

- The strong and powerful are to be envied; the humble and meek are to be scorned.

You and I have had to deal with these satanic influences coming into our lives day after day from all directions. Some of us unknowingly invite these influences into our lives because we cannot stand the thought of someone taking advantage of us or getting ahead of us.

But Jesus Christ said that the greatest among us would be the servant of all (Mark 10:44). That is God's truth on the matter, and it is up to us to recognize and apply that godly principle to our lives.

The only way you ever come into true life is by giving your heart and your life to serve others instead of yourself. Only by humbly bowing your knee in every situation will you find the promotion that comes from God. The Bible says that as you humble yourself under the mighty hand of God, He will exalt you in due time (1 Peter 5:6).

We are not in the middle of a game, friend; this is serious business. As Christians, we don't have the option of saying, "I'll do the right thing today if I don't feel too much pressure from my flesh" or "I'll do the right thing as long as it is comfortable to me." That's what the devil wants us to do. But the truth is, we've been listening to Satan tell us, "If it feels good, do it" for too long. We've even kept indulging in sin when it didn't feel good anymore!

As soon as you realize rebellion and disobedience are not the way—as soon as you begin to walk in the way of the Lord in obedience, trusting that He will take care of you no matter what situation you are in—things will change for you. You will not have to protect yourself any longer, for the Greater One will protect you. The Lord Jesus Christ will touch you in ways you cannot yet imagine. All you have to do is to choose obedience rather than follow your own agenda in life.

An Epidemic of Covert Rebellion

Rebellion is often manifested in our modern society in covert rather than overt ways. For instance, many employees find ways to be covertly rebellious because they want the paycheck at the end of the week. They don't want to get in trouble, so they make sure they cross their t's and dot their i's on the outside while they secretly undermine the employer's authority by gossiping or violating company policies, among other negative things.

Marriage is another institution that is being poisoned by rebellion. A wife who is in rebellion to her husband's authority in the home will usually find covert ways to rebel. After all, her husband is stronger than she is, so she doesn't want to face the confrontation that comes with blatant rebellion.

Another example of the rebellion that permeates our society is in the arena of civil authority. Many people think they can say whatever they want to say against their civil authorities. However, most people will go only so far in their rebellion because they don't want to land themselves in jail.

The truth is, there seem to be boundaries that constrain rebellion in every arena of society except one—the local church. The church is the one place where unscriptural forms of love and forgiveness are given in response to rebellion.

Paul stated about rebellion in the church of Corinth: "We are ready to punish all disobedience, whenever your obedience is complete" (2 Cor. 10:6 NASB). The apostle Paul couldn't properly deal with the rebellion that existed in the Corinthian church because so many in the congregation had been drawn away and seduced from the truth. So he told them, "As soon as I can get all the rest of you on the right side of the boat, we are going to see who the real problem is in the church; then we'll be able to deal with those people accordingly." Until the majority of the congregation was in proper submission to the authority in the church, there was absolutely no way Paul could do anything about the source of the rebellion.

The Galatian church is another example of this problem. If you remember, the church of Galatia had turned against Paul. Every time he'd go into that church, the people would be set free, God would perform miracles, and the Holy Spirit would move in the meetings. But the Judaizers always came right on Paul's heels to convince the church to side with them as they tried to prove that he was wrong. (See Gal. 2:4.)

The Galatian Christians believed the Judaizers. Turning away from the very person whom God had sent to set them free and help them, the Galatians gravitated toward their old religious ways once again. This happened with Moses again and again. In Deuteronomy 34:9 the Bible tells us that the people hearkened unto Joshua and did everything the Lord commanded Moses. During the lifetime he led the children of Israel, they gave him very little pleasure. In all actuality it was their rebellious attitudes that kept him out of the promised land.

This is what I mean when I say rebellious people who resist their proper authority cast off the allegiance that God has given to them for their benefit. They refuse to submit. They resist and oppose any level of control over their actions or their lives.

The fact is, there is a great need for a proper exercise of leadership in the arenas of the workplace, the home, the government, and the church. God has given the right to exercise authority within scriptural boundaries for a very good reason. It is heaven's way to prevent rebellion and disobedience from taking control and causing destruction in our lives.

You see, rebellion is in our genes. It is inside us. We have to understand how to overcome rebellion; otherwise, it will short-circuit any chance we have to experience God's success in our lives. And if left unchecked, rebellion will eventually destroy us.

Proverbs 5:9–14 confirms the consequences we will face if we choose to be rebellious:

> Lest you give your honor to others,
> And your years to the cruel one;
> Lest aliens be filled with your wealth,
> And your labors go to the house of a foreigner;
> And you mourn at last,
> When your flesh and your body are consumed,
> And say:
> "How I have hated instruction,
> And my heart despised correction!
> I have not obeyed the voice of my teachers,
> Nor inclined my ear to those who instructed me!
> I was on the verge of total ruin,
> In the midst of the assembly and congregation."

This person had almost come to ruin in the midst of the congregation. Why? Because he didn't obey God's commandments. And when he didn't obey, he didn't win. We learn from Isaiah 1:19–20:

> "If you are willing and obedient,
> You shall eat the good of the land;
> But if you refuse and rebel,

You shall be devoured by the sword";
For the mouth of the LORD has spoken.

If you rebel, you shall be destroyed. There are no ifs, ands, or buts about it. Obedience is better than sacrifice.

REBELLION LEADS TO DECEPTION

Rebellion is a trap that opens us up to deception and hinders us from living in the fullness of the blessings that God has provided for us. When we are in the clutches of rebellion, few of us recognize it. It can be very difficult to understand what is happening to us. If someone tells us that we are in rebellion, we often react in absolute denial and say, "You have to be kidding." Or even accuse those who bring it to our attention of being controlling or not allowing us to follow the Holy Spirit. What's worse is when those who truly want to obey the scriptures are accused of being cultish because they do not want to obey.

The enemy blinds us to our rebellion by getting us to focus on a falsely perceived truth. You see, life is lived by different perspectives. Each of us has our own perspective of life, and each of us believes our perspective is right. None of us approaches life thinking we are wrong about anything. We begin every day thinking we are building upon a ground-level foundation of truth.

Most of us don't consciously decide to be rebellious. We don't wake up in the morning and think:

- I can hardly wait to rebel today.

- I can hardly wait to mess up someone's life.

- I can hardly wait to be unfruitful in the tasks I am supposed to accomplish today.

- I can hardly wait to make someone mad.

- I can hardly wait to tick off my boss.

- I can hardly wait to have my spouse tell me that I am in rebellion.

- I can hardly wait for my spouse to say that I never show love to him (or her).

- I can hardly wait to yell at my kids because they didn't do what I told them to do.

- I can hardly wait to have God shake His fist at me in frustration.

People don't go through life with the understanding that their belief system is actually hurting them instead of helping them. Most don't realize that the very things they have embraced and clung to as truth are taking them down the wrong road.

Why is this? Because rebellion causes people to think that everyone else is wrong. The rest of the world may need to be adjusted, but they are all right. They are doing just fine. They have figured out the "right" way to live.

I see the deception that rebellion brings when some people talk to me about their employers. I find it a bit humorous when someone tells me that his boss doesn't know anything and that he is the only reason the company he works for is doing well. Others complain that a boss has the job they are supposed to have and that they have a right to be upset about not getting their deserved promotion. But whether they realize it or not, these people are in rebellion!

This deceptive trap of rebellion can be seen in every aspect of today's society. A wife submits to someone else's husband. A husband looks at someone else's wife and daydreams about how married life would be better with her. Church members look at another pastor and think, *He knows more than our pastor.* People continually want to hear something from someone else who has no stake in their lives.

Many times teenagers say they don't like what their parents tell them, so the kids go to someone else's parents to receive the guidance and advice that only their parents can give them. This, too, is rebellion.

You see, in every arena of life, God has chosen a way through authority for you and me to hear from Him and to be touched by Him. That's why God said, "Don't touch My anointed." Who is "the anointed"? To the employee, it is the employer. To a child, it is his parents. To a wife, it is her husband. To a husband, it is the Head of the church, Jesus Christ. To Christ, it is the Father (see John 16:13–14).

Insurrection is actually a posse of rebellious people who get together to "touch the anointed"—in other words, to undermine those in authority. In years gone by, I have experienced this type of group rebellion. I would walk down the hallway and hear these words inside my heart: Walk the plank, Mr. Christian. That made me aware that clandestine meetings were taking place in offices. Mutinous words were being spoken that were nothing less than Proverbs 30:20 (NASB) in action:

> This is the way of an adulterous woman:
> She eats and wipes her mouth,
> And says, "I have done no wrong."

The adulteress does wrong, then says she did not do it. People sow strife against their proper authority, then say they did not do it.

People live by all sorts of false perspectives, but only God's perspective is right and true. For instance, Sarah stood unseen behind the wall when the Lord told Abraham that He would visit her and that, within a year, Abraham would be holding a son. When Sarah heard that, she laughed silently to herself, and the Lord wanted to know why she laughed. She protested, saying that she didn't laugh, but the Lord replied, "Yes, you did laugh."

The problem wasn't that Sarah laughed. She really wasn't mocking the Lord; it just hit her as a bit humorous that a woman who was eighty-nine years old might become pregnant. According to Sarah's perspective, she didn't actually laugh. But the Lord said, "Laughter is what it was" (Gen. 18:15). You see, any given situation is not what you and I think it is. It is what God says it is.

We've seen that rebellion deceives people. Rebellion always justifies its own disobedience and causes a person to think everyone else is wrong. Rebellion points an accusing finger at someone else and accuses another for what is evil in its own heart. This deception is very seductive, but its grasp is choking; its sting is deadly; and few ever return from its burial vault.

Rebellion makes Christians think they're so smart that they are justified in rising up against the God-given authority on their job. As a result, God cannot move the way He wants to in that business. Sometimes these same people act as mentors in rebellion to their coworkers, causing them to move on and not accomplish the real reasons God had them at that position in the first place. Being there prepares them for the true place God has designed for them from eternity past. This cannot be accomplished until they have been faithful in another man's life (Luke 16:10–12).

Other Christians love to go to churches where they are more "spiritual" than the pastor so they don't have to submit to him (or so they think). They can just sit in the pew and tell themselves that they have their act together and that, as soon as everyone else gets straightened out, things will be better.

Satan is happy when he convinces you to sow rebellion in its various forms. He knows that whenever you sow rebellion, you will reap rebellion. He is very aware that there are seasons of disappointment in our future.

For instance, if you ever attain a position of leadership, you will want to have submitted people around you. But how can you reap submission when you haven't sown submission? You can never receive submitted people working for you if you were once a rebellious employee and you've never repented for your rebellion. You need to get before God and make it right. Get that rebellion out of your heart instead of trying to justify it to yourself.

You see, the devil wants you to think that you know more than anyone else and that you have a handle on things. He wants you to sit back and sneer and say, "That message on rebellion is for someone else, not me." But the moment you say that is the moment you have done the very same thing you have accused others of doing. You may not realize you are in rebellion, but it's true nonetheless.

THE SOURCE OF REBELLION

Do you know why the devil is such an expert at ensnaring people in his trap of rebellion? Because he is the very source of rebellion. Isaiah 14:12–14 (KJV) tells us how it all started for him:

> How art thou fallen from heaven, O Lucifer, son of the morning! how art thou cut down to the ground, which didst weaken the nations! For thou hast said in thine heart, I will ascend into heaven, I will exalt my throne above the stars of God: I will sit also upon the mount of the congregation, in the sides of the north: I will ascend above the heights of the clouds; I will be like the most High.

Five times Satan (then called Lucifer) said, "I will." Rebellion always says, "I will. I will do what I want to do. I will tell you what I think. This is what matters to me. This is how I see it. This is the way I think it should go."

But in Deuteronomy 8:17–18, God talks to the one who says, "I will":

Then you say in your heart, "My power and the might of my hand have gained me this wealth." And you shall remember the LORD your God, for it is He who gives you power to get wealth, that He may establish His covenant which He swore to your fathers, as it is this day.

In other words, God is saying, "Don't think that the might of your hand, your great learning, or your powerful anointing has attained any of the blessings you enjoy."

Satan's kingdom continually urges, "Protect yourself; do for yourself; look out after number one. Smite, smash, kill, devour, hate, beat, cheat, and steal from anyone who gets in your way." Some of these demonic principles have found their way into the church of the Lord Jesus Christ.

You can operate by these demon-inspired principles and not even know it. For instance, after you have been hurt by other people enough times, you may decide, I'm not going to put up with that anymore. I'm finally going to be someone who takes care of myself. But by deciding to protect yourself, you have taken yourself out of the protection that God has placed over your life.

One aspect of that divine protection is found in the designated authority of one's parents. Too many Christians prematurely take themselves out of this particular realm of protection. Others have removed themselves from the protection of their country's civil authorities, their authorities in the workplace, or the authority God has placed over them in their local church.

I believe that each decision leads to rebellion, causing a

malfunction in a person's life that eventually results in an inner dysfunction. The person then becomes exactly what Satan became when he said, "I will. It's my choice. No one can tell me what to do. No one can rule over me."

The truth is, all acts of rebellion from the cradle to the grave originate in the rebellion described in Isaiah 14. That includes man's very first act of rebellion in the Garden of Eden.

God commanded Adam and Eve to keep and dress this Garden. In the middle of the Garden was a tree that God told them not to partake of; if they did, they would die.

But then Eve came to the forbidden tree and conversed with the serpent. The devil gave Eve the idea that partaking of the tree would make her and Adam like God. Satan began by saying, "Has God said?"

You see, deception always sows suspicion in order to bring about rebellion. Suspicion must precede rebellion.

Satan asked, "Has God said? Did He really say that? He couldn't mean that you'd die if you ate of this tree. God knows that in the day you eat thereof, you will be as He is, knowing good and evil!"

Do you realize that Satan was tempting Eve with exactly the same thing he had desired in Isaiah 14—to be as God is? In the same way Satan had rebelled in heaven, he was causing man to rebel on earth. He first deceived Eve, and that deception gave birth to rebellion.

That's why James 1:22 cautions, "Be doers of the word, and not hearers only, deceiving yourselves." If you are a hearer of the Word and not a doer, you are deceiving yourself. You are like a man who looks at himself in a mirror and says, "I know what the Word of God says about me. I am the righteousness of God in Christ. I am healed by the stripes of Jesus. God has made me prosperous. I am a winner and not a loser. I am not what I look like; I am not a product of my past. I am not looking at all those generations that have gone before me. I am what God says I am!"

But then this man doesn't follow through on that confession of faith. Because he takes no action on those truths of God, the Bible says he forgets what manner of man he is. He has become a hearer and not a doer of the Word, and now he is on dangerous ground. If he doesn't start having active obedience and submission in his heart and life, his complacency will ultimately breed rebellion.

So remember—don't make the mistake Saul did when he yielded to pressure from those below him in order to answer the One above him. Never ask those below you how you can be obedient to God. You must do whatever you have to do to obey God without bowing to the desires of those below you. Don't look to them for your obedience. Be obedient to God and His Word.

And don't be submissive only when it's agreeable to your flesh. It doesn't matter that your husband leads the family in a way that he shouldn't. It doesn't matter that your boss seems clueless about what he is doing. It doesn't matter that your pastor makes mistakes as he tries to lead the congregation. These things do not give you the right to rebel. God will deal with those above you if they exercise their authority in the wrong way. He just wants you to have a submitted heart. There is something that must be discussed for a moment. We must always keep in mind that we are not submitting *to* a person we are submitting *through* a person. When I face the injustices of a recalcitrant authority figure instead of resisting and rebelling against them I raise my standards to a level that is far beyond their expectations. In so doing I under promise and then over perform. In the case of a wicked superior I obey up to the point where they are requiring me to disobey the written word of God but even when they expect me to disobey the word of God my attitude is one of submission while I obey God. Submission is a heart attitude not a physical obedience. This is clearly seen in Shadrach, Meshach, and Abed-Nego.

You may be tempted to justify yourself whenever you try to buck those in authority over you. That's what Saul did. Rebellion and disobedience always try to justify themselves.

People who are rebellious always think they are a prize. They can fall into rebellion and still think they are doing the right thing. Why? Because they are being destroyed for lack of knowledge. They have yet to discover that it is the word of God that they submit to and not to people.

When you think you know something, you are finished. But when you think you know nothing, God can use you. I have watched this for a long time, and I know what I'm talking about. So don't wait another fifteen years to figure out how to forsake rebellion. Listen to someone who has already left where you are now and has reached where you want to go!

WHAT IS REBELLION?

We must first define rebellion so we know what it is. In Webster's 1828 dictionary, rebel means to revolt; to renounce the authority of the law and government to which one owes allegiance; to rise in violent opposition against lawful authority. According to

Strong's Concordance to rebel is to cause to make bitter or unpleasant; to resist and provoke; to disobey grievously; to change. This is what rebellion is in God's eyes. With this in mind, let us take a look at some biblical examples.

THE REBELLIOUS ISRAELITES

Another characteristic of rebellious people is that they are difficult to handle. They are always resisting and opposing, always sowing doubt and contention, always needing to be ministered to. (That's why God looks for people who are "easy keepers." These are the people He can use!)

For instance, Exodus 32 relates Moses' situation with the rebellious Israelites. Moses had climbed the mountain of God to meet with God face-to-face. As the days went by and the people waited for Moses at the foot of the mountain, they became impatient. They complained to Aaron the high priest, "Moses delivered us out of bondage in Egypt, but he's been gone a long time. We don't know what happened to him. We want something to worship that we can see, Aaron. Make us gods that will go before us in the wilderness!"

Aaron yielded to the people's pressure and made them a golden calf to worship. When Moses and Joshua came down from the mountain, they heard the people dancing and singing in celebration of their new "god." Joshua said, "It sounds like the roar of victory in war."

Moses replied, "This is not the cry of victory or defeat; it's the sound of singing."

When Moses saw what the people were doing, in anger he

threw down the stone tablets upon which the finger of God had written, breaking them into pieces. Then Moses asked Aaron about the golden calf. Aaron responded,

> Do not let the anger of my lord become hot. You know the people, that they are set on evil. For they said to me, "Make us gods that shall go before us; as for this Moses, the man who brought us out of the land of Egypt, we do not know what has become of him." And I said to them, "Whoever has any gold, let them break it off." So they gave it to me, and I cast it into the fire, and this calf came out. (Ex. 32:22–24)

Aaron said he didn't do anything wrong; it was the people's fault. This is the response of rebellion—always pointing an accusing finger at someone else. It wasn't the last time the Israelite people would prove to be rebellious and difficult to handle—a "stiff-necked people," as God aptly called them (Ex. 32:9). And the Bible tells us that they paid a high price for their rebellion, for their names were blotted out of the Book of Life forever. Only Joshua and Caleb were able to enter into the promised land.

SAMSON VS. JOSEPH

Let's look at another biblical example of rebellion and its consequences. We can see the symptoms of rebellion in the life of Samson (Judg. 13:24–16:31).

Samson had a problem in his life. In the beginning, he was anointed. His father was a priest, and Samson was called to be a

Nazirite, separated unto God to be a deliverer of Israel from their enemies, the Philistines.

But one day Samson told his father to obtain for him a certain Philistine woman to be his wife because he had seen her and she pleased him. His father yielded to his son's pressure, even though he knew Samson was not to marry an unbelieving wife.

This unlikely match started a series of events in which Samson would perform great feats against the Philistines in retaliation for the wrongs they committed against him. One time he tied the tails of three hundred foxes together two by two; then he sent the foxes into the Philistines' cornfields with lighted firebrands stuck between each set of tails. Another time Samson killed a thousand Philistine men with the jawbone of an ass!

However, Samson performed all these feats from a foundation of deception and rebellion. As a result, he never fulfilled his divine call to deliver Israel, and he ended his life blind and in bondage. (Samson's rebellion centered on what he saw with his eyes, and in the end, his eyes were gouged out by his enemies.)

Now contrast Samson's life with the life of Joseph. Joseph was not a Nazirite. He was not anointed. He wasn't anything except submitted.

We'll talk more about Joseph later, but right now let's note some basic facts about his life (Gen. 37:1–47:27). Joseph received a coat of many colors from his father, Jacob, who loved him dearly. Life was good—until his jealous brothers sold him as a slave to the Ishmaelite traders. Those traders then sold him to an Egyptian man named Potiphar.

Potiphar's household was blessed because of Joseph, and

Joseph performed his work with such excellence that Potiphar promoted him in no time at all. Then Potiphar's wife lied about Joseph because he wouldn't yield to her seduction, and he was thrown in jail.

Even in jail, Joseph was submitted. Soon the keeper of the prison gave him authority over all the other prisoners in the jail. While in prison, Joseph correctly interpreted the baker's and the cupbearer's dreams.

Later Pharaoh had a dream of seven fat cows and seven lean cows, seven fat ears of corn and seven lean ears of corn. No one could interpret his dream for him but Joseph, the one who would not bow down before any other god or compromise with his God.

As a reward for his service to Pharaoh, Joseph became the second in command of the greatest nation in the world at that particular time. He not only saved his family from starvation and obliteration, but also saved an entire lost nation, making it the richest nation of its time.

Joseph accomplished all this through submitting. On the other hand, Samson, who was anointed, lost his anointing because he disobeyed the One in authority over him.

DON'T SMITE THE SHEPHERD

Submission and accountability bring promotion from the Lord. The reason many of us have not been promoted is that we have not dealt with our rebellion. God doesn't put people in our lives in positions of authority so we can turn up our noses at them. He puts them there so we can honor Him and demonstrate our love for Him as we submit with a willing heart.

Zechariah 13:7 (KJV) warns, "Smite the shepherd, and the sheep shall be scattered." When we smite those who are in authority, everything in life begins to break down. For instance, when we smite our president (with rebellious words of criticism), the country experiences a general breakdown in respect and moral order. That's why Romans 13:1 teaches us: "Let every soul be subject to the governing authorities. For there is no authority except from God, and the authorities that exist are appointed by God."

God put in place every authority on this earth. However, God put in place the position of authority, not the person. Therefore, it is our responsibility to respect the office or position that has been delegated by God, not necessarily the person.

Even when the person in authority does poorly in his role of exercising authority, we don't have the right to rebel. First Peter 2:18–19 states,

> Servants, be submissive to your masters with all fear, not
> only to the good and gentle, but also to the harsh. For this
> is commendable, if because of conscience toward God one
> endures grief, suffering wrongfully.

Even if you have a bad boss, submit yourself to him as an act of obedience to the Lord. God put that authority in place so you could be exalted.

How does this principle apply to the home? If you are a wife and mother, you need to realize that your children believe whatever you tell them about your husband. You spend more time with your children than your husband does. During the time you spend with your children every day, you can tell them anything you want to about their father. You can "smite" your husband with words of criticism that your children will believe, even if their father is wonderful to them when he comes home from work. As a result, a scattering—a disintegration of unity, peace, and godly order—will take place within the family unit itself.

When you smite the authority in any arena of life, those underneath that authority will be scattered. At that moment, you sign the papers that say where you are right now is as far as you will ever be exalted in life. By your act of rebellion, you have sprung the devil's trap, opening the door to an unwelcome visitor whose only goal is to destroy you.

· Chapter 3 ·

GOD'S WAY OF RELATING TO AUTHORITY

Saul was a man of rebellion, and we have seen the consequences he suffered for his disobedience. On the other hand, David knew how to relate to authority according to God's ways. David was a man of submission. He kept his heart right before God and never rebelled against Saul, no matter how many wrongs the king committed against him. David's willingness to relate correctly to his God-ordained authority was a big reason why God called David a man after His own heart.

LEVELS OF AUTHORITY

Let's talk about God's way of relating to authority. First, we must understand that God requires everyone to be under authority. His whole Book is about relating to authority.

God has established certain levels of authority that each and every one of us lives with and that we can never renounce or avoid. He has set these authority levels in His Word for our protection.

When believed in and built upon, these levels of authority will make a profound and beneficial difference in all our lives.

I can say that my life has been enriched by every level of authority that God offers. Let's find out about these primary levels of authority.

1. God

Exodus 20:1–17 records what are known as the Ten Commandments. I don't consider them so much the Ten Commandments as the Ten What Will Happens. In other words, the Ten Commandments warn us what will happen unless we give ourselves completely to God.

For instance, the very first and most important commandment is this: "You shall have no other gods before Me" (v. 3). God has to be Number One in your life, the primary One you are interested in pleasing and obeying. This is the mandatory foundation for relating correctly to all other levels of authority in life.

2. Parents

The second level of authority that God gives us is the authority of our parents. God has delegated authority to our parents so they can raise us up in the way we should go. With that in mind, consider Ephesians 6:1–3:

> Children, obey your parents in the Lord, for this is right. "Honor your father and mother," which is the first commandment with promise: "that it may be well with you and you may live long on the earth."

This passage of Scripture tells me very simply that if I always show honor to my parents and maintain an amicable relationship with them throughout my life, things will go well with me, and I will live long upon the earth.

Yet these verses are being increasingly disobeyed in today's world. The greatest breakdown in our society over the past thirty years has been the breakdown of the home, whether in the relationship between husband and wife or between parent and child.

You may be a product of rebellion. Maybe you were born in the sixties or seventies, and you relate to Diana Ross's song "Love Child." You may have begun to sow seeds of rebellion in your own life. If this is the case, don't spend your time wondering why negative things are happening to you. You are only reaping what you have sown.

But remember, God always gives you a way out so you may be able to stand against the temptation to rebel and not give in to the pressures of life. You can't change yesterday, but you can change tomorrow.

As a parent, you are your children's authority until the time they get married. After they are married, you then become their counselor. As your children's counselor, you should continue to impart positive things into their lives. This is something you must get across to your children at all times. God has given you authority in their lives, and He will bless them through the authority He has given to you.

A child or a teenager may look obedient on the outside when he is actually nursing rebellious attitudes on the inside. But God has given parents the gift to see beyond any false actions of obedience to their children's hearts where rebellion lies.

You see, it isn't just a matter of your child biding his time and keeping your rules until it's time for him to leave home. What matters is not his actions, but his heart. It's as simple as that. Never forget that if you discipline your attitudes you will never have to discipline your actions. As a parent, you understand that your children will make mistakes. Everyone makes mistakes. No one is perfect. But one situation you shouldn't tolerate is knowing that your child is rebellious in his heart, even though he is obedient in his outward actions. If you have nothing to jump on his case about, ask God for a way to draw out that rebellion so you can deal with it scripturally. Don't allow rebellion in your children to fester unchecked.

Be careful about sending your children off to be on their own or to enroll in an institution of higher learning that will rip out all the godly principles you've instilled in them over the years. You do your best to give your children a solid foundation of love, wisdom, and knowledge to help them succeed in life. But too often children allow rebellion to take over in their lives before that wisdom can take root. They start thinking they can make it on their own.

You may think your kids need to know how to live outside the home before they get married. But Genesis 2:24 (NASB) instructs, "For this cause [getting married] a man shall leave his father and his mother, and shall cleave to his wife; and they shall become one flesh."

"For this cause"! God did not say, "Just because you want to live downtown, you shall leave your father and mother." Until your children get married, you are to provide the authority they need to help them enter into the real world and succeed in life. Make sure you don't abandon that God-ordained role of authority prematurely!

3. Husbands

If you are a wife, you may think, *I've got the raw end of the deal in this marriage. I have to submit to my husband, but he can do anything he wants and get away with it.* That just isn't true. Your husband has to submit to a God you cannot see. And I guarantee you this: God's standards for your husband are a lot higher than your husband's standards are for you!

When God wants something done, He doesn't tell your husband that he's doing fine if he isn't. If it isn't perfect, He just says, "Do this again. This isn't the way I wanted it done."

God isn't like your husband, who might say to you, "Sweetie, you really did a good job ironing my shirt. I appreciate that so much." Meanwhile, he's thinking, Of course, you always make a crease in my shirts in the wrong place because you think I like it that way. But I can't say anything about it because every time I open my mouth to give a little constructive criticism, you take it wrong and get upset!

God doesn't deal with your husband that way. He is straightforward in His correction and exacting in what He requires of him. So I recommend that you enjoy your role as a wife. Even though your husband may not be perfect, he does not require of you what God requires of him.

4. Employers

One of the greatest things your employer can perceive about you as an employee is that your heart is the same as his. When he knows your heart is submitted to his authority and his goals for the business or company, he knows that he never needs to worry about you. He can rest in the knowledge that you will be just fine.

When this is the way your employer perceives you, you may not hear from him a lot, but don't let that make you feel neglected. It isn't that he has nothing to say to you. He just has to spend most of his time taking care of the rebellious employees who are difficult to handle! Rest assured; your value as an employee has been noticed.

5. Government

Romans 13:1–7 talks about the governmental authorities that God has given us to obey. Verse 1 starts out with this statement: "Let every soul be subject to the governing authorities. For there is no authority except from God, and the authorities that exist are appointed by God."

You may say, "Wait a minute! Do you mean to tell me that every one of our country's presidents has been ordained of God?" No, I didn't say that. God has put the framework of governmental authorities in place, but He doesn't put every person in that position of authority. In most cases, the person is chosen by the people as they operate within the framework God has established.

Romans 13:2–6 continues,

Therefore whoever resists the authority resists the ordinance of God, and those who resist will bring judgment on themselves. For rulers are not a terror to good works, but to evil. Do you want to be unafraid of the authority? Do what is good, and you will have praise from the same. For he is God's minister to you for good. But if you do evil, be afraid; for he does not bear the sword in vain; for he is God's minister, an avenger to execute wrath on him who practices evil. Therefore you must be subject, not only because of wrath but also for conscience' sake. For because of this you also pay taxes, for they are God's ministers attending continually to this very thing.

Not only do you obey these governmental authorities because you are afraid of what may happen if you don't, but you also obey for conscience' sake. Then when Satan tries to insert rebellion into your life, you can tell him, "No, devil! I haven't sown rebellion, so I won't reap rebellion. You can't put that on my children, my marriage, or my job. You can't put rebellion in any area of my life!"

6. Church

As far as Jesus was concerned, Peter was a leader who needed to encourage his friends to continue to go on with God. That's why Jesus told Peter, "I have prayed for you, that your faith should not fail; and when you have returned to Me, strengthen your brethren" (Luke 22:32).

With that in mind, let's read what Peter wrote to the church in 1 Peter 5:1–5:

The elders who are among you I exhort, I who am a fellow elder and a witness of the sufferings of Christ, and also a partaker of the glory that will be revealed: Shepherd the flock of God which is among you, serving as overseers, not by compulsion but willingly, not for dishonest gain but eagerly; nor as being lords over those entrusted to you, but being examples to the flock; and when the Chief Shepherd appears, you will receive the crown of glory that does not fade away. Likewise you younger people, submit yourselves to your elders. Yes, all of you be submissive to one another, and be clothed with humility, for

"God resists the proud,
But gives grace to the humble."

Church leaders may readily give up on people who will not act the way God wants them to act or submit themselves to the local church. But in reality, the problem goes back much farther than these people's refusal to submit to the church. The source of rebellion for many church members can be traced back to the second level of God-ordained authority—the authority of their parents. I have never met a rebellious church member who has had a good relationship with his or her parents.

But the truth is, to find the true source of the problem with rebellious church members, we should back up all the way to the first level of authority—God Himself. These people are not rebelling against the church as much as they are rebelling against God.

God said that when you rebel against Him, you will run yourself aground. Once again, let's consider His warning in Isaiah 1:19–20:

> "If you are willing and obedient,
> You shall eat the good of the land;
> But if you refuse and rebel,
> You shall be devoured by the sword";
> For the mouth of the Lord has spoken.

The writer of Hebrews had something to say about how we are to relate to our authorities within the local church: "Obey those who rule over you, and be submissive, for they watch out for your souls, as those who must give account. Let them do so with joy and not with grief, for that would be unprofitable for you" (13:17).

God is telling us to do two things in this verse. First, He tells us to obey. This word obey is unqualified because God trusts Himself. He is saying to us, "If you will obey your leaders within the church, I will deal with them regarding anything that needs to change."

Then, God tells us to submit ourselves to those who have the rule over us. The definition of the word submission is "the act of putting one's will underneath the will of another." But please keep this in mind: the word submission is not synonymous with the word agreement. In fact, submission never comes into play until there is no agreement. Only when all hopes of agreement are gone does submission kick in!

You see, obedience is an action, but submission is an attitude. For instance, your child may take the garbage out of the house whenever you ask him to, but it can become a real drag to have to get on his case to do it. The child tells you that he took out the garbage. What he doesn't say is that he did it just to avoid a major fight. In other words, he obeyed, but he didn't submit. If he had taken out the garbage willingly, you wouldn't have had to say a word to him. He would have done it of his own volition out of a submitted heart.

Now think about how you would feel if your child took out the garbage without your even knowing that he had done it. You just noticed later that the garbage was gone when you looked under the sink. Wouldn't you want to find a way to bless your child for his willingness to obey? Certainly you would. Well, that's how God feels about you when you both obey and submit to those who have rule over you.

God also says the person in charge within the church must give an account of those under his authority. He then exhorts the church member to make sure his leaders are able to give an account of him with joy and not with grief, for that would be unprofitable to him.

Notice that the Bible does not say that a person's lack of submission would be unprofitable to his church leaders. It says it would be unprofitable to the person who is being rebellious. All hope for profit and blessing in a person's life is lost when he does not submit himself to the authority that God has placed over him in the church.

I remember one time I got into an area of rebellion in a church because of a lack of knowledge. At the time, I wasn't able to recognize the rebellion I was in. Once I did recognize my error, however, I called that pastor on the phone and begged him to forgive me. He laughed and tried to brush it off as no big deal. But I said to him, "Pastor, I am begging you to forgive me for the rebellion I showed all those years ago in my life. I didn't know; I wasn't aware of it. But it was wrong, and I need to ask you for forgiveness."

These are the six primary levels of authority that God has designed to benefit and profit us in our lives. But we receive the benefits only as we choose to relate His way to each of the authorities He has placed over us.

GOD SPEAKS TO THE ONE IN AUTHORITY

The values of the society in which we live have crept into the church of the Lord Jesus Christ to the point that the local church has often turned into an "opinion center." Members of the congregation decide whether or not they like certain decisions the pastor is making or certain things he is doing. They have the idea that these issues are open for discussion. But they are not open for discussion as far as God is concerned!

This principle was in operation when Moses married an Ethiopian woman and his older sister and brother, Miriam and Aaron, became upset about it and talked to each other about the situation.

> Then Miriam and Aaron spoke against Moses because of the Ethiopian woman whom he had married; for he had married an Ethiopian woman. So they said, "Has

the LORD indeed spoken only through Moses? Has He not spoken through us also?" And the LORD heard it. (Num. 12:1–2)

You see, Miriam was a prophetess, and Aaron was the high priest—the number one priest of the most high God. Every priest had to be of Aaron's lineage in order to become a priest. Aaron and Miriam thought their prominent positions among the Israelites gave them the right to rebel against Moses. They thought they were justified in asking, "Has the Lord spoken only through Moses?" But they were about to find out that they were wrong!

I wish I could give you a quarter of a penny for every time I have heard someone ask, "Has the Lord spoken only through the pastor?" If I did, then you, your family, and the people on your block could retire forever!

When rebellion sets in, some people grumble and say things such as, "How does the pastor know what is best for us? All he is trying to do is to manipulate and control us." They didn't think I was controlling when they wanted to know the answers. I became "controlling" only when they decided they didn't want to know.

Let's find out what happened when the Lord heard the grumblings of Aaron and Miriam:

(Now the man Moses was very humble, more than all men who were on the face of the earth.) Suddenly the LORD said to Moses, Aaron, and Miriam, "Come out, you three, to the tabernacle of meeting!" So the three came out. Then the LORD came down in the pillar of cloud and stood in the door of the tabernacle, and called Aaron and Miriam. And they both went forward. (Num. 12:3–5)

Can you imagine what Aaron and Miriam were thinking? They probably thought, *Moses is finally going to get his! God is going to deal with him about marrying that Ethiopian woman. Moses knows better than to marry outside the tribe of Israel, and God is going to jump his case about it. We are finally going to be put in charge the way we should have been the whole time. We can't figure out why the youngster was ever put in charge, but today is our day!*

The Lord came down in the pillar of cloud and stood in the door of the tabernacle. Then He called for Aaron and Miriam, and they came forth.

Isn't it interesting that God stood in the doorway? He was blocking the door; Aaron and Miriam couldn't run out when He started talking to them! (So many times people change relationships and locations as soon as someone brings up something they don't like that could potentially help their lives. These people need someone to stand in the doorway for them!)

Listen to what the Lord told Aaron and Miriam:

"Hear now My words:
If there is a prophet among you,
I, the LORD, make Myself known to him in a vision;
I speak to him in a dream.

Not so with My servant Moses;

He is faithful in all My house.

I speak with him face to face,

Even plainly, and not in dark sayings;

And he sees the form of the LORD.

Why then were you not afraid

To speak against My servant Moses?"

So the anger of the LORD was aroused against them, and

    He departed. (Num. 12:6–9)

God asked Miriam and Aaron, "Why weren't you afraid to speak against the one whom I placed in charge?" You should remember that the next time you say something against your pastor. If I were you, I'd be afraid to do that because God is listening to you! Aaron and Miriam held very high positions within a body of three million people. And if God didn't like them talking against their leader, I'm sure He isn't happy with you doing the same thing.

God will always speak to the person who is in authority. That's why He wanted to know why Aaron and Miriam weren't afraid of talking against the anointed of the Lord. Why didn't fear grip them when they brought up his name in an unholy manner? Why did they not let what and who Moses was before God make a difference in their lives?

The answer is simple: rebellion challenges but submission changes. In challenging rebellion, I open the door to deception.

God will keep your secrets regarding certain things in your life over which He has given you authority. But I can tell you from personal experience as a pastor that, at times, He will speak to the person in authority over you concerning your life.

Sometimes I will be standing in the shower, and God will suddenly break into my thoughts and say, I want to talk to you about So-and-so. Or as I'm walking through my day, God will interrupt my morning and say, Excuse Me. (God can excuse Himself in my life anytime He wants to!) Then He tells me to call So-and-so and say thus and such.

I call the person on the telephone and say, "God has told me to tell you something. Now, I really don't know you well. I have no knowledge concerning you in the natural, but I think you are wonderful. You are the best thing since sliced peaches! All I am telling you is what I have been told by the Lord. He is watching you. He is dealing with you. Don't spurn the chastening of the Lord in your life. Be open for God to touch your life."

Perhaps you have been guilty of rebellion against your boss, your parents, or your pastor. Maybe you got offended, and now you're upset. You think you should be able to voice an opinion, even if it pertains to an area over which God has not given you authority.

But you should never attempt to take authority over something for which God has not given you the responsibility. For instance, God never made you responsible for those in authority over you. He told you to do something for them, but He never told you to take responsibility for them. If they do something wrong, He is the One who will deal with them.

When Aaron and Miriam tried to deal with Moses, the "anger of the LORD was aroused against them, and He departed" (v. 9). God was upset with them, and He let them know about it.

> And when the cloud departed from above the tabernacle, suddenly Miriam became leprous, as white as snow. Then Aaron turned toward Miriam, and there she was, a leper. So Aaron said to Moses, "Oh, my lord! Please do not lay this sin on us, in which we have done foolishly and in which we have sinned." (Num. 12:10–11)

Aaron said that speaking against those whom God has placed in charge is sin. It is rebellion against the word of the Lord. So Aaron had to go to Moses, God's chosen leader, and ask him not to lay the guilt of their sin upon them. Aaron pleaded with Moses:

> "Please do not let her be as one dead, whose flesh is half consumed when he comes out of his mother's womb!" So Moses cried out to the LORD, saying, "Please heal her, O God, I pray!" (Num. 12:12–13)

The Lord answered Moses' prayer and healed Miriam. But first, she had to spend a week in the lepers' camp, learning firsthand about the dire consequences of rebellion against her God-ordained authority.

Refuse to speak against your leaders in the Lord. I don't care how wrong they are; you are never to speak against those God has placed in authority over you.

Besides, did you ever think that you might be the one perceiving the situation incorrectly? Maybe in two weeks you'll get the revelation that your leader is right. But by then, it might be two weeks too late.

Decide never to speak against God's leader, no matter who he is or what he does. Never.

I have made my decision. I will not speak against God's person in authority, no matter who he is. God has made him, called him, and anointed him. Whatever he does wrong, God will deal with him.

BARNABAS'S ERROR
IN RELATING TO HIS AUTHORITY

Did you ever feel that you had reached a place in life where you could go no farther? Has it seemed as if an invisible glass ceiling is keeping you from ascending into what God has planned for your life? Well, I want to talk to you about Barnabas. If you've been wondering why you haven't been promoted in life, Barnabas's story might very well be your answer.

Barnabas is another biblical example of someone who rebelled against his God-ordained authority. The incident I'm talking about is found in Acts 15:36–40:

> After some days Paul said to Barnabas, "Let us now go back and visit our brethren in every city where we have preached the word of the Lord, and see how they are doing." Now Barnabas was determined to take with them John called Mark. But Paul insisted that they should not take with them the one who had departed from them in Pamphylia, and had not gone with them to the work. Then the contention became so sharp that they parted from one

another. And so Barnabas took Mark and sailed to Cyprus; but Paul chose Silas and departed, being commended by the brethren to the grace of God.

Everyone knew about and loved Barnabas. He was nicknamed "the son of encouragement" and had earned a glowing reputation with all the churches. But Barnabas made a grave error in this particular situation when he refused to submit to the leadership of his senior authority, the apostle Paul.

Paul spoke to Barnabas regarding his plans to visit the people they had ministered to up to that point. Barnabas mentioned that he wanted to take John Mark with them, but Paul wasn't agreeable to that suggestion. Paul reminded Barnabas of the time they were in the heat of the battle back in Perga of Pamphylia (Acts 13:13). When things got hot, John Mark left them to go back to Jerusalem.

Barnabas wanted to forgive John Mark and act as if the young man had never abandoned them. He wanted to promote John Mark before he was prepared for this level of ministry. But Paul said no. He told Barnabas that he would not entrust the ministry team to that type of attitude.

According to the Bible, the contention became so great between Paul and Barnabas that they broke up the team and went separate directions. Barnabas would not yield so Barnabas took John Mark and went on his own missionary journey. Meanwhile, Paul chose Silas as his companion and continued with his plans to visit the new churches where he had previously ministered the Word.

From that point, we hear nothing else about Barnabas

throughout the rest of the book of Acts. His name seems conspicuously left out, never to be mentioned again. Why is this? Because false love gave birth to rebellion in Barnabas's life.

DON'T RUN AWAY
FROM YOUR SEASON OF PRUNING

Barnabas's reaction when Paul refused to take John Mark along shows that Barnabas didn't understand the biblical principle of pruning. You see, we all have seasons in our lives, just as the earth does—seedtime and harvest, summer and winter. During the earth's winter season, impurities are killed in the ground so it will be ready to bring forth new life in the spring. The same thing happens during the winter seasons of our lives. This is the time of pruning, when God cleanses us of impurities that hinder our walk with Him.

In John 15, Jesus talked about this process of divine pruning:

> I am the true vine, and My Father is the vinedresser. Every branch in Me that does not bear fruit He takes away; and every branch that bears fruit He prunes, that it may bear more fruit. (vv. 1–2)

I used to read these verses and think, *What in the world is Jesus talking about here?* I finally get to the place where I think I am looking good and "fruity." I think I have my act together. Then all of a sudden, God begins to cut things out of my life!

But later I came to realize that God does this so we can bear more fruit. We need to embrace the times of "branch snapping," especially when the pruning originates with those God has placed in authority over us.

We need to get to the place in our lives where we don't break our relationship with our authorities in times of tempest. We should make sure we continue to receive everything we are supposed to receive in those relationships as we submit to the pruning of the Lord.

Let's suppose you are a member of my congregation, and we develop a friendly relationship. All of a sudden, God begins to deal with me about your life. He tells me to talk to you about an area of your life that needs to change. He knows that the only way you will get the sin out of your life in that area is to have someone minister to you about it because you aren't listening to Him.

What are you going to do when God begins to point His finger at certain areas of your life? I'll tell you what most people do—they get offended. The next thing they do is to talk against the leader who confronted them with their problem. At this point, these people are going down the tubes because they will not receive the chastening of the Lord. However, they aren't going alone. They share their concerns about the leader with other people. Now they are taking a number of other individuals down with them.

People have the idea that the chastening of the Lord is designed to make you angry, but it is actually designed to make you grow. Perhaps the reason you have never been promoted is that you have never received the Lord's chastening. You may say that you want to submit to those who are in authority over you in the church. But every time you "get in the doorway," you opt out and say, "It's too hot in the kitchen!"

What am I talking about? Well, maybe your pastor tells you:

- "By the way, you need to get your relationship with your spouse straightened out."
- "You need to ask your children's forgiveness for taking out your frustration and anger on them."
- "You need to make it right with your boss for usurping his authority."
- "You are killing everything good in your life with your rebellion. When are you going to do something about it?"

If you start feeling the heat, don't run. Receive the Lord's chastening in humility, for there is blessing on the other side!

My friend, I am talking to you about things that make you win in life. The body of Christ in America has lived for too long a "cotton candy" style of Christianity, focusing on God's sweet message of grace and forgiveness and largely ignoring His command to live in holiness and humility.

MAKE SURE YOU'RE RUNNING ON THE RIGHT FUEL

You know, a lot of Christians today call Jesus their friend when, in reality, Jesus doesn't even want to hang around with them! You and I must qualify for the friendship of Jesus. In Proverbs 13:20 Solomon said, "He that walks with wise men shall be wise but a companion shall be destroyed." We must remember that Jesus ministered to tax collectors and sinners, but it would be a huge hypocrisy if Jesus hung around with those God told him not to. Jesus doesn't take the term friends lightly. He said in John 15:15: "No longer do I call you servants, for a servant does not know what his master is doing; but I have called you friends." Jesus walked with His disciples on an intimate basis for three and a half years before He called them friends.

You can never be a friend to those in authority over you until you are first a servant. This is true at all levels of authority. Linda could never have become my wife unless she had first served my life by answering a problem for me. The same is true with my relationship with Jesus. Until I answer a problem for Him, I cannot be His friend.

Jesus called Judas His friend. For three and a half years, Judas was faithful. For three and a half years, Judas used God's principles. But then Judas tapped into the fuel that makes Satan's kingdom run: rebellion.

Remember, the number one commandment in the satanic bible is "do what you want to do." The Bible talks about that satanic principle when it says, "Everyone did what was right in his own eyes" (Judg. 17:6).

When someone becomes involved in satanism, the first thing the cult members do is to get the person loaded on drugs and alcohol. A person who is on drugs can be controlled. Next, they get the person involved in a tremendous amount of illicit sex. All of this draws the person into deep, deep rebellion.

Just as rebellion is the fuel that makes Satan's kingdom run, obedience to God and to delegated authority is the fuel that makes His kingdom run. This is also true in the natural realm. In any organization, you don't receive a promotion unless you are obedient to your authority within that organization.

Not enough can be said about this principle, of which Saul is the classic example. When God anointed Saul king, he was a humble man. But Saul came to the place where he began to think he could do no wrong. He began to do things his own way, contrary to the word of the Lord given to him through God's mouthpiece, the prophet Samuel. In other words, Saul began to run his kingship on the fuel of rebellion, and it cost him his kingdom.

Today you can hold the Word of God in your hands. You can read it anytime you want to, or you can close it and it will shut its mouth to you. God leaves it completely up to you whether or not you rebel against His delegated authorities in your life. But I guarantee you—if you choose the devil's way of relating to authority instead of God's way, you will be the loser in the end.

Entrust Yourself to Him
Who Judges Justly

No one can make you submit instead of rebel because submission is a "want to." It is your choice. God told you to submit to those who have rule over you. Now it's up to you whether you heed that word of the Lord.

I want you to imagine a "thoroughbred" Christian who has tremendous potential that God wants to use for His kingdom. This person is trained by a faithful minister for three years so he can be effectively used by God. But one day this person gets the idea that he wants to go off on his own and do his own thing. Not only has that person chosen rebellion or slow spiritual suicide, but he has also taken three years off the life of that faithful man of God and thrown it down the devil's tubes!

This happens throughout the body of Christ, and it grieves the Father's heart. God calls certain believers to hook up with the vision of a minister. But instead, these believers decide to go off on their own. They think everything is cool, but it isn't. The minister in charge cannot fulfill the vision in his heart as effectively as God intends—all because those who are under his authority have decided that God wants them to do something on their own.

God never called anyone to be by himself. He designed the body of Christ to be givers, not takers—to deposit and not to withdraw; to submit and not to rebel.

What if I believe I am supposed to do something with all my heart and the people in authority in my life tell me no? As far as I'm concerned, the answer is no.

You may ask, "Do you mean to tell me that if God tells you to do something and those in authority over you tell you no, you won't do it?" That's right. I'd say, "God, I love You, and I know You love me. I know that You can talk to this person in authority if You want me to do this."

I cannot pick and choose when I think my authority hears and when he doesn't. Once I have locked in my commitment to submit, that's it; I'm in.

I'll use my marriage as an example. Suppose I don't do something right in my role as a husband, and Linda tells me, "That's it! Either do that right, or I'm quitting this marriage!" Neither Linda nor I can live our lives that way. Why? Because that is the response of rebellion.

God tells us to obey those who have rule over us. So what do we do if the person in authority starts leading us into something that we question in our hearts? We must first remember that if someone asks us to sin, God's word takes precedence over this type of request. But in most cases, this is not the objection of the believer. Most of the time we will suffer as Jesus did so this is our response. First Peter 2:23 gives us the key by describing Jesus' response to the wrong actions of the religious leaders of His time: "When they hurled their insults at him, he did not retaliate; when he suffered, he made no threats. Instead, he entrusted himself to him who judges justly" (NIV).

We should do the same thing Jesus did if those in authority over us start leading us in the wrong direction: we need to entrust ourselves to God and ask the Father who judges justly to change them or change the situation. God will always protect us and deliver us when we entrust ourselves to Him.

But what if we don't hold fast to this elementary biblical principle of submission to God-ordained authority? Then Christianity is nothing more than a nice club to belong to. The moment that we don't believe what God says about obeying those who have rule over us is the moment that we believe our opinion is more important than God and that our feelings are more important than His Word.

The truth is, we can trace every failure in our lives to a violation of this principle through rebellion. Satan said he was going to ascend to the sides of the north and exalt his throne above God's throne. God said, "No, that isn't going to happen. But as far as Satan wanted to go up, that is how far he is going to go down."

The same thing happens to us in our lives. The farther up we think we will go on our own, the farther down we will go because of our rebellion.

GOD'S REQUIREMENTS IN RELATING TO AUTHORITY

God has three major requirements that you must fulfill in relating to authority. First, you must be in right standing with God and with your delegated authority; second, you must remain under God's umbrella; and last, you must be concerned for your authority's reputation.

STAY IN RIGHT STANDING WITH YOUR AUTHORITIES

We read in Psalm 66:18: "If I regard iniquity in my heart, the LORD will not hear." Don't think for a moment that God is going to continually answer your prayers while you actively choose to stay in sin and rebellion. He will not do it. His promises come to you with the condition of obedience.

Remember, Romans 13:1 (KJV) states, "Let every soul be subject unto the higher powers. For there is no power but of God: the powers that be are ordained of God." "Every soul" includes you, so this verse is talking to you. You are to be subject to the higher powers. There are higher powers in life than you. You must subject to those higher powers because you are not beyond making an error in judgment. No one is.

All of us are capable of making mistakes because we can make decisions based only on the information at our disposal. That's why we can be destroyed through lack of knowledge. One of the ways God has given us to gain the knowledge we need to be blessed is to listen to our "higher powers"—the authorities He has placed in our lives.

So here are some questions to ask that will help you locate yourself regarding how you relate to authority:

- Am I under authority, or am I only maintaining the outward form of a good attitude?

- Have I put my trust in God regarding the authorities who are over me?

- Do I have a clear conscience regarding how I relate to my authorities?

- Am I negative and critical about any of the authorities God has placed over me?

I realize that Paul said in 1 Corinthians 6:11 that God has washed you and set you free from the guilt of sin. But you still have a responsibility to maintain your right standing with God and His delegated authorities in your life.

Here are a few more questions for you to answer:

- Have I truly put myself under the authority of my employer at my job?

- Do I have a clear conscience when I go to work in the morning?

- Do I really believe that I am doing what God wants me to do and that I am where God wants me to be?

These are tough questions! Answering yes to these questions may seem an almost insurmountable goal to you. However, once you achieve that goal, you will avoid many unnecessary struggles of many people because they won't put themselves under authority in the workplace.

Now ask yourself these questions:

- Have I really put myself under the authority of the church?

- Do I have a clear conscience when I come to church, or do I come in and start spreading gossip or speaking words that hurt people's faith?

- When I talk to the church elders, am I really listening to what they say, or am I just conning them?

You know, many people want their pastor to be their friend, but they don't really want him to act as their pastor. I believe friends are important. But if a believer receives a friend in the name of a friend, he receives a friend's reward. If he receives a pastor in the name of a pastor, he receives a pastor's reward.

You can have a lot of friends, but you can have only one pastor. Therefore, I strongly suggest that you go for the greatest reward you can receive. How do you do that? By willingly submitting yourself without reservation to your pastor and the other leaders in your church.

Let me give you one final question to ask yourself regarding this subject of maintaining your right standing with God and His delegated authorities:

- Have I done what I have been asked to do by my authorities? Is my conscience clear about this?

Why do I keep asking you if you have a clear conscience? Well, read Ephesians 6:13–14: "Having done all, to stand. Stand therefore." If you don't have a clear conscience regarding how you relate to authority, you can't stand strong in faith. The devil can trick you. He will say that things are not as they should be in your life because of all the rebellion you've never dealt with.

The devil keeps telling people things like that day after day after day, putting them under a cloud of condemnation and guilt. That's why it's so important to maintain a clean conscience and to make sure you've done everything your authorities have asked you to do.

STAY UNDER GOD'S UMBRELLA OF PROTECTION

What are the consequences of rebelling or of relating poorly to those whom God has placed over us? Proverbs 17:11 tells us:

> An evil man seeks only rebellion;
> Therefore a cruel messenger will be sent against him.

Once again, there will be times when you see deficiencies in your spouse, your boss, and your pastor. You will always see what you consider to be examples of failure in their lives. But if you allow the deficiencies to determine your obedience to that authority, you will open up your life to Satan and take yourself out from underneath the umbrella of protection that God has given to you.

Christians used to talk a lot about this umbrella of protection back in the 1970s. But there is an important truth in this concept. If you leave the parameters of God's Word, you take yourself out from under His protection and leave yourself open to get beaten up by the devil. Don't do it! Just decide that you're going to stay underneath the authority God has placed over you.

We are talking about a level of truth here that very few of us ever attain: the surrender of our hearts to God in every area of our lives. I have personally come to that place in my walk with God. I have prayed: "Lord, I want to learn how to submit to You. I want to surrender myself to Your will. I want to learn how to submit to You in my home. I know I am responsible to You, not to my wife, regarding how I lead my family. I am responsible to You, not to my congregation, regarding how I lead the church."

You see, every responsibility goes upward, not sideways. I am responsible to take care of and lead the church I pastor according to the Word of God, no matter what that means. Even if it means hurting myself, I have to obey the Word. If I want to walk closely with God in every area of my life, I can't decide to "fake it till I make it." There is no way to win the heart of God and stay within His protection by faking a submitted heart!

BE CONCERNED FOR YOUR AUTHORITY'S REPUTATION

You can see why God is so interested in cleansing us from all traces of rebellion: "Having these promises, beloved, let us cleanse ourselves from all filthiness of the flesh and spirit, perfecting holiness in the fear of God" (2 Cor. 7:1). Holiness does not refer to morality here. Holiness and morality are not synonymous. Holiness has to do with the way we relate to other people and the way we relate to authority in our lives.

I can tell you this: if I had not submitted to the God-ordained authorities in my life over the years, I would not be standing in the position of ministry that I hold today. That is the truth. I have never knowingly raised my hand against my authority in the spiritual arena. I thank God that I never did!

When it comes to relating to the authorities under which God has placed us, we must have a pure heart. Proverbs 22:11 explains why:

> He who loves purity of heart
> And has grace on his lips,
> The king will be his friend.

The king here can refer to anyone who is in a position of delegated authority. Leaders are looking for people who possess a pureness of heart.

What does it mean to have a pure heart toward those in authority over you? It means you are concerned for their reputation.

A good name is to be chosen rather than great riches,
Loving favor rather than silver and gold. (Prov. 22:1)

Let each of you look out not only for his own interests,
but also for the interests of others. (Phil. 2:4)

Never let people say whatever they want to say about those who are in authority over you. Do all you can to protect their reputation. Otherwise, you run the risk of losing the benefits God has planned for you to receive through that delegated authority.

If you allow anyone's words to come against the person who taught you faith or your delegated authority in the Lord, your faith will not work for you again until you make it right before God. You will still know the right words to say, but there won't be any life in those words. You will try as hard as you can, but your faith will be as good as dead because you came against your delegated authority in God.

In that case, it doesn't matter how slick you think you are. The devil will eat you for a snack! In fact, your "slickness" will wear off only when (1) you choose to submit your heart or (2) you have a face-to-face confrontation with the devil and find out you have no power in your life.

I don't let people talk negatively about my wife—not even my son. My son may have a little bit of trouble with his mother sometimes, but he will not walk around with "that face" concerning my wife. That is the way God planned it; that is the way He wants it to be; and that is how we are going to live. No one is going to show disrespect toward my wife if I have anything to say about it.

A failure to live this way is part of the reason why some children prefer one of their parents over the other. They know they can come to the preferred parent and get whatever they want. They don't see their parents as a unit.

It doesn't work that way in our home. If Linda says anything to our son, the question is not what Dad thinks. That question was answered a long time ago. Dad thinks whatever Mom said. If my son wants to negotiate with me, he should do it before his mom ever voices her opinion. I am not going to decide with my son over my wife. There is no chance of that. If she is wrong, she and I will discuss it after he is disappointed. He will never know of her making one mistake in my eyes because I am concerned for her reputation.

You can see Moses' concern for God's reputation in Deuteronomy 9:26–28. Moses was pleading with God not to destroy His people. God told Moses to get out of the way because He was going to mow them down with His heavenly "lawn mower."

Moses said, "God, do You know what everyone will say about You if You do that? Do you know the kind of reputation You will get?" As a result of Moses' pleading his case for the Israelites and for the Lord's reputation, God relented and showed mercy to His rebellious people.

So always be concerned for the reputation of those in authority over you. Instead of "pulling down their drawers" in public, make sure they have a whole bunch of clothes on!

Help Fulfill Your Authority's Goals

Your relationship with your authorities is based on your relationship with God, not with other people. It doesn't matter what anyone else thinks. What God thinks is all that matters. Therefore, another important part of maintaining a pure heart is to do everything possible to help fulfill the dreams and goals of those in authority over you.

I used to walk into my boss's office almost every day at the parcel delivery service where I worked and say, "Boss, I just want to let you know one thing. I consider it my personal responsibility to get you a promotion. I am here to fulfill everything your boss would ever expect from you. I want you to have an easy day. I want to let you know that I am not someone who is out there stealing from you or trying to make any money off the company. I want you to know I am out there today doing the best job I can. You can use me as an example of someone who wants to fulfill the dreams and goals of the one for whom he works."

He'd answer cynically, "Yeah, sure, Robb."

Bosses come and go when they get promoted, so I had more than one boss at that company to whom I said that. For some of those bosses, I had to use my faith in order to see them the way God sees them. I didn't like those particular bosses very much as people, and they didn't like me. But I'd still say, "Boss, I am here today to get you a promotion."

"I really don't like you, man."

"I don't care about that," I'd say. "Whether you like or dislike me, love or hate me, it doesn't matter to me. Today I am here to get you a promotion."

Now, one of two things was going to happen to me as I continued to do that for those problem bosses. God was going to shoot me up to the top by promoting me, or the bosses were going to start leaving me alone.

According to Acts 5:13, the worldly people dared not join themselves to the early Christians. The world both feared and highly esteemed the followers of Jesus. I faced a similar situation at my parcel delivery job. My coworkers were afraid of me! There were sixty drivers in my division, and none of them knew what to do with me. They didn't mess with me, and neither did my bosses. Meanwhile, I just kept doing my best to help those in authority over me get a promotion!

If you are in a position of authority, imagine what it would be like to have someone say to you every day, "I am here to get you a promotion today." When people say that to you, the burden of responsibility suddenly falls off you to find a way to get ahead. You don't have to try to please the right people. The people under your supervision are there to help you.

This is why your boss looks for people with a pure heart to work for him. He doesn't want a bunch of people who go to work only to put in their eight hours. He isn't interested in employees who work only three hours and gossip with their coworkers the other five.

When I went to work at that parcel delivery company, I didn't go to develop relationships with people. I went to work to work. When I received a paycheck, the name of one of the other drivers wasn't written at the bottom. The boss who signed the bottom of my check was the one who had my attention. I was there to make him famous.

Do you know what happens when you have that kind of pure-hearted attitude toward your authorities? You get famous! The people in authority over you start seeing you as someone who helps them solve their problems and accomplish their goals. And as God blesses them, He will also bless you.

Always offer positive input at work. Be someone your boss can count on. Don't let him think for one moment that once he teaches you everything he knows about the business, you will be heading down the trail. If he did think that way, do you think he would put the time into teaching you everything? I don't think so. He doesn't want to spend every day feeling paranoid and eating Tums. He is looking for someone he can trust.

You can be that person. God has given you delegated authorities to bless you and exalt you in life. You can be the faithful person they are looking for because of your pureness in heart.

Always Uphold the Authority of Those Over You

Finally, maintaining a pure heart means always upholding the authority of those over you. No matter what happens, you uphold their authority.

Once a person has achieved something, he wants people under his supervision to help him maintain the level to which he has achieved. For instance, a journeyman carpenter doesn't want to do the "grunt's" work. He wants to work with a good grunt who will stick with him and won't quit after working for him a week, forcing the journeyman to do the menial labor at the expense of excelling even more in his craft.

All people in responsible positions feel this way. That's why they want the people who report to them to uphold their authority rather than try to take it away.

Always be concerned for the reputation, goals, visions, and authority of those whom God has placed over you in life. And realize this: the devil cannot get into any area of your life where you decide to uphold authority—whether it is the government, the workplace, your home, your parents, or your church. Satan cannot influence you when you have a submitted heart; he can influence only rebellion. And rebellion is able to creep only into the areas where you fail to uphold authority.

I'm talking about the making of a person who walks in excellence in this life, my friend. These qualities should come forth from your heart and cause you to be head and shoulders above all your contemporaries.

No one achieves a promotion by complaining and criticizing. People in positions of authority don't want to hang around you if you are full of strife. But you can learn how to relate to authority God's way. You can become the kind of person your authorities are looking for—a person of submission with whom they can share their hearts and give their full trust.

· Chapter 4 ·

CHOOSE OBEDIENCE

The Jews in the temple looked over in wonder at the unusual sight. A man whom they recognized as the lame beggar from the Gate called Beautiful had just entered the temple with two men. But he wasn't lame anymore. He was walking and jumping about in joy as he shouted praises to God!

The scene caused a great stir. A crowd gathered around the three men at Solomon's Porch. They watched as the healed man held on tightly to his two companions as a drowned man would to his rescuer.

The two men standing with the once lame beggar were Peter and John. Seizing the opportunity, Peter started preaching to the crowd about the risen Jesus who had caused this lame man to be healed. Soon the religious leaders and temple police came running over to silence and arrest the two disciples.

But the members of the Sanhedrin were in a fix. They couldn't downplay this notable miracle that everyone had witnessed. The best they could do was order the disciples not to preach anymore in the name of Jesus.

> Peter and John answered and said to them, "Whether it is right in the sight of God to listen to you more than to God, you judge. For we cannot but speak the things which we have seen and heard." (Acts 4:19–20)

More miracles happened in the days that followed as Peter, John, and the other apostles continued preaching about Jesus. The religious leaders had the apostles arrested and put in jail again, but their prison stay didn't last long. That night, an angel of the Lord opened the jail doors and commanded them, "Go, stand in the temple and speak to the people all the words of this life" (Acts 5:20).

Peter and the other apostles left the prison and kept obeying the word of the Lord. Once more they were arrested as they preached about Jesus; once more they were brought before the Sanhedrin to give account for themselves. The high priest asked them, "Did we not strictly command you not to teach in this name? And look, you have filled Jerusalem with your doctrine, and intend to bring this Man's blood on us!" (Acts 5:28).

Peter and the other apostles weren't intimidated by the religious leaders. They replied with confidence founded in knowing the One they served: "We ought to obey God rather than men" (Acts 5:29).

You see, obedience is ultimately unto God, not unto man. We obey through the authorities of our lives, not to the authorities of our lives, and we obey even when it isn't convenient to us.

People Who Obeyed God
in Hard Times

I want to talk to you about a few other people in the Bible who obeyed God. These people were obedient even when it wasn't convenient—even in the midst of severe hardship.

Let's start with Sarah. We already saw what happened when Sarah was eighty-nine and the Lord visited her and Abraham's home. She overheard the Lord say that she would be holding her own son within a year. She laughed within herself at the thought that God would come through for her in such a supernatural way.

Nevertheless, God still called Sarah a woman of faith: "By faith Sarah herself also received strength to conceive seed, and she bore a child when she was past the age, because she judged Him faithful who had promised" (Heb. 11:11).

Sarah's faith can also be seen in how she related to her husband, Abraham. Even though Abraham twice tried to give her away to another man out of fear (Gen. 12; 20), she still chose to obey him as her authority: "Sarah obeyed Abraham, calling him lord" (1 Peter 3:6).

If God said that Sarah must call Abraham lord, she would do it in obedience to Him—not based on what her husband had done but based on what God had said.

Abraham, too, was a man of obedience: "By faith Abraham obeyed when he was called to go out to the place which he would receive as an inheritance. And he went out, not knowing where he was going" (Heb. 11:8).

When God tells you to go out and do something, He knows

exactly where He's sending you. He has everything already set up for you to succeed if you are obedient.

Now, you may say you don't want to be obedient to God. Well, neither did the devil. You may not think you should be obedient to God, and you don't have to. You can do whatever you want. You can go to hell if you want to! No one is making you go to heaven. If you want to burn, you can go ahead and get crispy! It's your choice.

As we saw before, Joseph was a man who obeyed God. Sold as a slave to Pharaoh's servant Potiphar, Joseph went into Potiphar's house and started doing better than any of Potiphar's other servants. Everything to which Joseph put his hand prospered in his master's household. Potiphar saw that Joseph was wise and therefore promoted him to the position of overseer of his house. However, the esteem, respect, and admiration Potiphar's wife felt for Joseph eventually turned to lust. Since he was her slave, she thought he would do what she told him to do.

Potiphar's wife told Joseph to come and lie with her. But even though Joseph was her slave, he told her, "I will not do that to my God" (Gen. 39:9).

This answers a question you might have regarding the delegated authorities in your life. The authorities are there only because of God. Therefore, should any one of those placed in authority over you ever try to make you disobey God, that person is actually uprooted from his position of authority. The position is still there, but the person is gone.

The prophet Daniel is an excellent example of a man of obedience who had to choose God over his delegated authority.

Daniel 1 tells the story of how Daniel fared better than the people of Nebuchadnezzar's household. Instead of eating the delicacies that belonged to the king, he ate only fruit and vegetables in obedience to the law of his God. Yet in the end, Daniel came out sharper in mind and healthier in body than all the rest of them!

Later Daniel's rivals turned on him and convinced King Nebuchadnezzar to make praying to God illegal. A royal decree was brought forth that people could pray only to the king's image.

But that didn't stop Daniel from praying to the God of Israel. One day his enemies found him praying and took him to Nebuchadnezzar. Against his will, the king put Daniel in the lions' den. Because Daniel obeyed God instead of Nebuchadnezzar and kept praying, he was delivered from that lions' den unharmed (Dan. 6:4–23)!

JESUS' EXAMPLE OF OBEDIENCE

The word obedience means "giving in to the orders or instructions of one in authority or control" (*Webster's New World,* Second College Edition). It implies one who gives himself to obeying by choice. The Hebrew word is *shama,* which means "to listen intelligently; to be attentive; to respond favorably; to consent."

Jesus is our best example of all of Someone who was completely obedient to the Father. Hebrews 5:8 (KJV) speaks of this: "Though he were a Son, yet learned he obedience by the things which he suffered."

You see, when you come to a place of uncompromising obedience toward the Lord and the authorities He has placed in your life, a tremendous heart wrenching takes place within you at times. Why? Because obedience is not convenient. It isn't necessarily happy either. It is not always what you want to do or what the world has taught you to do.

Jesus understood this well. You see, Jesus had to learn how to say no to His flesh the same way you and I do. He didn't grow to maturity and finally go to the cross without ever having to deal with His flesh. He had to learn how to obey God. Jesus had to learn how to turn off His body, turn off His mind, and turn off what He thought was right because of all the information He had gathered throughout His lifetime. He had to say no to all that and yes to God.

Consider what Paul said about Jesus:

> For if by the one man's offense death reigned through the one, much more those who receive abundance of grace and of the gift of righteousness will reign in life through the One, Jesus Christ . . . For as by one man's disobedience many were made sinners, so also by one Man's obedience many will be made righteous. (Rom. 5:17, 19)

Jesus was actually obedient in order to make you and me righteous.

Because of Jesus' obedience, the apostle Paul went on to make this appeal to us:

> Do not present your members as instruments of unrighteousness to sin, but present yourselves to God as

being alive from the dead, and your members as instruments of righteousness to God. (Rom. 6:13)

You and I choose to whom and to what we will be obedient. We make the choice.

The choice that wins the heart of God is obedience unto Him. That means you don't spend your time trying to figure out how much sin you can commit and get away with. If your heart is obedient to God, you don't allow yourself to wonder:

- How much of what Satan has spoken can I get away with and still be okay with God?

- Can I speak disrespectfully about my delegated authorities?

- Can I raise a question about my authorities' ability to lead?

- Can I criticize my parents?

- Can I raise a question about my boss's management skills at work?

- Can I bring up accusations concerning my civil authorities?

- Can I complain about how it is so hard to serve God?

- Can I drag down the leadership in the church of the Lord Jesus Christ and sow my seeds of discontentment in others' lives until it destroys their faith?

Instead of dwelling on these negative thoughts, your mind becomes preoccupied with the desire of your heart—to draw closer to God through obedience to Him.

HOW TO BECOME MORE OBEDIENT

How do you become more obedient to God? First, you must know that God is the supreme Ruler of all. What He says takes precedence over what you feel. As we are told in Proverbs 3:5–6:

> Trust in the LORD with all your heart,
> And lean not on your own understanding;
> In all your ways acknowledge Him,
> And He shall direct your paths.

In every situation, fall into God's arms.

Second, hearken diligently to God's voice. Joshua 1:8 tells you why:

> This Book of the Law shall not depart from your mouth, but you shall meditate in it day and night, that you may observe to do according to all that is written in it. For then you will make your way prosperous, and then you will have good success.

Third, bring your mind and body under subjection to God. This is a must. Paul declared, "I beat my body and make it my slave so that after I have preached to others, I myself will not be disqualified for the prize" (1 Cor. 9:27 NIV).

You must make your body your slave so that you are not a slave of your body—in other words, a slave to your carnal passions or to the pressures and disappointments of life.

Fourth, make your thoughts think what God thinks. Every one of your thoughts should be obedient to Christ.

> I beseech you therefore, brethren, by the mercies of God, that you present your bodies a living sacrifice, holy, acceptable to God, which is your reasonable service. And do not be conformed to this world, but be transformed by the renewing of your mind, that you may prove what is that good and acceptable and perfect will of God. (Rom. 12:1–2)
>
> Casting down arguments and every high thing that exalts itself against the knowledge of God, bringing every thought into captivity to the obedience of Christ. (2 Cor. 10:5)

It doesn't matter what I know, what I think, or what anyone says. All that matters is this: Is this thought in line with what God says about the situation?

The reason many people never perform well or accomplish much in life is that they allow their minds to think thoughts that are off-limits with God. I have made the decision that I'm not going to do that. I refuse to entertain thoughts that are contrary to what God says.

For instance, if you sat and thought about adultery all day, every day, it wouldn't take a month before your body would obey your mind. Or if you thought about robbing a bank again and again, you'd eventually try it, no matter how dumb the idea sounded or how sure you were that you couldn't pull it off.

This arena of the mind is the source of most Christians' problems. They think they are going to overcome the devil after spending most of their time meditating on their problems and the opinions of the world. But it just isn't going to work. It's like leading a charge on hell with a water gun!

Here's one more guideline for becoming more obedient to God: give Him control of your money. Isn't that an interesting thought? To be obedient, you must give God control of your finances.

Jesus emphasized this point in Matthew 6:19–21:

> Do not lay up for yourselves treasures on earth, where moth and rust destroy and where thieves break in and steal; but lay up for yourselves treasures in heaven, where neither moth nor rust destroys and where thieves do not break in and steal. For where your treasure is, there your heart will be also.

To give God control of your money, you must do what He says about tithing:

> "Bring all the tithes into the storehouse,
> That there may be food in My house,
> And try Me now in this,"
> Says the LORD of hosts,
> "If I will not open for you the windows of heaven

And pour out for you such blessing

That there will not be room enough to receive it." (Mal. 3:10)

These are all crucial steps to becoming more obedient to God. But remember, obedience takes away all your excuses and arguments. To obey God, you must be "argument free" because obedience doesn't have anything to do with what you think. Obedience hearkens only to what God says.

When you finally come to the place in your life where you are obedient to God, no matter what He tells you to do, you will be on the path to winning His heart. Instead of arguing or rebelling when God tells you to do something, you will yield out of love for Him. Instead of resisting, you will entrust yourself to His wisdom. Instead of twisting His arm to try to find out why He wants you to do it, you will speak from a submitted heart: "Nevertheless, not my will, but Yours be done, Lord."

· *Chapter 5* ·

GOD'S ONLY PATH TO FULFILLMENT

I'm so confused. I don't know what I should do with my life. My pastor shared with me some ways to find out God's will, but I want to do what I want to do."

"I'm so frustrated with my job. I am convinced my boss doesn't know anything! I certainly know more than he does. The best way to handle this is for me to do my job my way instead of his because I know I can do it better than he can."

"Your parents want you to be home by 10:00 P.M.? You have to be kidding me. You are not going to do that, are you?"

"My husband wants me to listen to a tape and meditate on the Word before I go out and spend social time with friends. He says our family really needs to build its foundation on the rock of God's Word. But I want to get going, so I'll do it later."

Do any of these statements sound familiar? Do any of them hit the mark in your life? I hope not because every one of these statements reflects one thing: an unsubmitted heart.

What thoughts come to your mind when you hear the word submit? If you are a husband, you probably don't like someone other than yourself telling your wife to submit. And you probably think you have said it so much that it means absolutely nothing to her! In today's society, submission has almost come to mean a self-centered husband using the Bible to make his wife into everything he wants her to become.

If you are a woman, the word submission may make the hair on the back of your neck stand up. You may despise the thought of anyone bringing up the subject in conversation.

If you are an employee, submission means you not only need to listen to your boss, but you need to do what he says and be happy about it.

If you are a child in your home, submission means that there isn't much room for discussion; you must obey your parents.

"But what happens if they are wrong?" a child may ask. "Why does it always seem that I have to be the one who submits?"

That last question is asked a lot. "What about my boss? What about my husband? What about my parents? What do they have to do? It seems that they are the ones who get angry, and I'm the one who gets disciplined! They get mad, and I get the rod. When do they ever get the rod? Who gives the rod to them?"

The truth is, submission touches every person in every walk of life, whether we realize it or not. But it is obvious that many people have the wrong idea about submission. Their concept of submission is often either archaic or distorted; as a result, people tend to miss what God meant when He used that word.

The apostle Paul talked to the church at Ephesus about

"submitting to one another in the fear of God" (Eph. 5:21). Peter said this about submission:

> Likewise you younger people, submit yourselves to your elders. Yes, all of you be submissive to one another, and be clothed with humility, for "God resists the proud,
> But gives grace to the humble." (1 Peter 5:5)

It seems we cannot see the forest for the trees when it comes to submission. We cannot see the forest because the leaves are blocking our view of how God designed us to be in our lives on this earth.

The truth is, the leaves hanging on those trees that keep us from seeing what God really has for us happen to be the same leaves Adam and Eve once sewed together to make themselves aprons! Most of us don't see the fine print of pride and self-centeredness written on those leaves Adam and Eve sewed together—fine print that reads:

- I want to be as God.
- It is all about me. It doesn't have anything to do with you.
- I want my way.
- No one will ever tell me what to do.
- I hear from God as well as my boss (my pastor, my husband, my father, etc.) does. Therefore, I am not going to listen to him.

You and I need to push past the leaves that block our view of the Father's heart and learn how to walk His only path to fulfillment: godly submission.

What the Centurion Understood

Matthew 8 tells us about a Roman centurion who is a key figure in this discussion about understanding the nature of true submission.

> Now when Jesus had entered Capernaum, a centurion came to Him, pleading with Him, saying, "Lord, my servant is lying at home paralyzed, dreadfully tormented." And Jesus said to him, "I will come and heal him." (Matt. 8:5–7)

This centurion called to Jesus for help, and Jesus replied, "I will come and heal him."

> The centurion answered and said, "Lord, I am not worthy that You should come under my roof. But only speak a word, and my servant will be healed. For I also am a man under authority, having soldiers under me. And I say to this one, 'Go,' and he goes; and to another, 'Come,' and he comes; and to my servant, 'Do this,' and he does it." When Jesus heard it, He marveled, and said to those who followed, "Assuredly, I say to you, I have not found such great faith, not even in Israel!" (Matt. 8:8–10)

The Twentieth Century New Testament translates verse 9: "For I myself am a man under the orders of others."

It was typical for a Roman centurion to believe he was superior to other people. Romans in general thought they were superior to Jews because the Roman Empire had taken over the entire known world at that time. Having conquered so many tribes and nations, the Romans thought they knew more and were a better class of people than anyone else.

In light of this fact, the account of this incident in Luke 7 tells us something profound: the Jews came on their own initiative from the synagogue, beseeching Jesus to help this centurion. They said, "Lord, this man is worthy for You to heal his servant, for he prays always and he has built us a synagogue." (See Luke 7:4–5.)

This centurion understood prayer. But he understood something else just as important as prayer. He said, "For I also am a man under authority, having soldiers under me. And I say to this one, 'Go,' and he goes; and to another, 'Come,' and he comes; and to my servant, 'Do this,' and he does it" (Matt. 8:9).

Matthew 8:10 notes what happened when Jesus heard the centurion's words: "He marveled, and said to those who followed, 'Assuredly, I say to you, I have not found such great faith, not even in Israel!'"

Why did Jesus respond the way He did to the centurion? I submit this thought to you: Jesus wasn't responding to the centurion as much as He was responding to all the people who were following Him. How many people were following Jesus at that time? We know there were at least twelve men. We also know that thousands of people could have been there.

Jesus saw something inside this centurion. The man came to Him recognizing something that others didn't recognize—something that 99.9 percent of all people never grasp their entire lives. Then the centurion responded according to that revelation of truth. That is why Jesus exclaimed to the Jews who were following Him, "I haven't found such great faith in all of Israel!" He was saying, "I haven't yet met a Jew who understands this."

What did this man understand? He understood that the emperor of Rome could give a command and it would be fulfilled to the farthest parts of the empire with no questions asked. Because the centurion was a man under authority, he recognized that the situation was similar for Jesus. Jesus carried out everything He did under God's authority.

In different settings, Jesus would speak of this divine chain of command. He'd say things like, "I do only those things that I see My Father do. I do those things I am told to do. What I see, that is what I do. What I tell the Holy Spirit, that is what He says. The Holy Spirit does not speak of Himself, but what He hears He shall also speak. He doesn't make up His own ideas of what to say."

The centurion understood this "chain of command" concept, so he told Jesus, "You only have to speak the word, and my servant will be healed." This righteous man knew that Jesus was speaking not of His own authority, but of the authority given to Him as He kept Himself in submission to His heavenly Father.

What Is True Submission?

I want to share with you the definition of submission I obtained from the 1927 edition of the New Century Dictionary. Submission is a "joyful yielding; to surrender; to resign." It refers to "a superior nature that bows himself low to someone else" and is an "equivalent to slavery." It also means "to abide by the decision of an authority; to resign oneself to the authority and will of another."

Submission does not mean that you are any less, that you are subservient, or that you are worthless, inferior, or a doormat for others to step on. Submission is never belligerent, defiant, or resistant. A submissive person does not take part in a revolt.

Submission is the insulation that God has given to us to keep us from eating consistently of the Tree of the Knowledge of Good and Evil. It is a means of divine protection—a form of spiritual insulation that keeps us away from things that will destroy us. Submission keeps us from pursuing positions of responsibility or prominence that God may have assigned to someone else.

Many people never learn to truly submit to authority because they live their lives in the area of agreement, not authority. These people have the idea that submission is nothing more than agreeing with those in authority over them. The moment they don't agree with their authority is the moment they don't submit. But as I noted before, people who have that concept of submission couldn't be more wrong.

If you want to win the Father's heart, my friend, you have to understand this: a submitted life doesn't start until agreement has come to an end. Submission and agreement do not have an equal sign between them. Submission doesn't even begin to have any type of meaning until there is disagreement. Only when a person disagrees with his authority does submission come into play.

That's why your flesh doesn't like to submit. In fact, you'll deal with this issue of submission versus agreement in every relationship with authority from the time you are a baby until the time you die. Whenever you don't agree, you will face the temptation to opt out of what God has designed for that relationship.

After I came to Christ was when I truly married Linda from my heart. I knew that my decision didn't mean I'd stay with her only as long as she was nice to me. I made the commitment to love her as Christ loved the church. However, there was nothing I could do to keep our marriage intact if she opted out.

My basic attitude when I proposed to her was this: "As for me and my house, we are going to serve God. That is the direction I am going, so if you want to go that direction, too, get on the train! If you don't want to, don't get on the train. It's that simple. But if you get aboard, look out because I am going to love you as Christ loved the church!"

Let me reiterate this vital point: people have the wrong idea that unless the authority to which they are supposed to submit is doing things "right," they should not submit. This happens whether the relationship is between child and parents, wife and husband, employee and employer, church member and church leader, or citizen and government official. People think, You said something I didn't like, so I am out of here!

Think about what happens in your relationship with your

children when they rebel. No matter how hard you try, you cannot speak into their lives. If you have a wife who is determined to be rebellious, there is nothing you can do about it. That's just the way it is. Or if you have a husband who is a "you know what," there is nothing you can do about that either.

You see, you can't determine whether or not another person submits to the authorities in his life. The only thing you can determine is whether or not you will submit to authority. Someone else's decision to submit to or rebel against authority shouldn't determine what you do.

SUBMISSION IN THE HOME

You are the one who has to say, "I choose to submit myself to the authorities whom God has placed in my life, and I will receive the benefits of these authorities. I won't try to make them be something other than what God has called them to be. I will receive only the reward that comes from God's anointing on their lives."

Let's talk about this principle in regard to the home. In 1 Corinthians 11:3 (KJV), Paul said this: "I would have you know, that the head of every man is Christ; and the head of the woman is the man; and the head of Christ is God." Paul just said everything he needed to say about marriage in one verse! You see, too often we expect our spouses to be what only Jesus can be to us. That expectation can lead to a real problem in the marriage and, if it is not corrected, can eventually lead to a broken home.

That's why I told my wife from the very beginning of our marriage, "I love you, but you don't take the place of Jesus in my life.

Whenever I have to choose between you and Jesus, He wins—but that means so do you!"

Ephesians 5:21–22 (KJV) explains how submission in the home should work: "Submitting yourselves one to another in the fear of God. Wives, submit yourselves unto your own husbands, as unto the Lord."

When you first begin a marriage relationship, there is a period of time when you are learning to submit yourselves one to another. During that time, you court each other; you take the time to get to know each other; and you watch to see how the other person lives his or her life.

To illustrate what I'm talking about, let me use the example of my job at the parcel delivery company. Of course, you need to keep in mind that my job at that company was a far cry from two people's commitment in a marriage relationship!

When I first decided I wanted to work for that parcel delivery company, I checked out whether it was a good job and how the management treated employees. For instance, I like clean uniforms. I like clean trucks. I don't like working with a bunch of slobs, and I don't want to be a slob. So before I even applied for a job, I did what I could to make sure it could fit into what I wanted for my life.

Then came the courtship time of my employment when I was learning to "submit myself one to another" with the rest of the people who worked there. Part of that learning process meant keeping my commitment level high even when I climbed into my nice-looking delivery truck and saw the dirty aluminum insides!

You see, when you keep your commitment level high, you also

keep your zeal level high. You can't expect other people to be the entertainment you depend on to keep your attitude right or to keep you strong and on top of things. When you always expect someone else to fill that role for you, you'll find yourself in trouble a large part of the time. Whenever that person has a bad day, so will you.

Most of the guys I worked with at that company complained all the time. They would wake up most mornings feeling discouraged. Those men eventually lost their jobs. To this day, some of them still make less money than they were making when they worked at that company years ago! Why? Because they didn't work on keeping their commitment and passion levels high.

The story of my life since those days as a delivery driver is quite different. I learned early on that commitment and passion are my responsibility in life, not anyone else's—certainly not my wife's! I don't go home in the afternoon and say, "Linda, I will put a quarter in you, and then you can entertain me. If you'll do that, I'll like you and think you're all right as a wife! However, in a couple of hours we will try this again, so don't get your hopes up that I will continue to like you."

That is exactly the way marriages operate when spouses try to control each other instead of submitting themselves to each other in the fear of God. They never give themselves the opportunity to know the person they married. They can never enjoy each other because they are always trying to mold the other person into someone they want him or her to be.

Remember that submission is not agreement. As the head of our home, I shouldn't have to play the game "Mother, May I?"

every time I have to make a decision. I should be able to count on my wife's support once I say, "This is the direction I believe our family is supposed to go."

Suppose a husband says this to his wife, and the wife doesn't agree with him. Two weeks later, he comes back and says the same thing. The wife still doesn't agree. Then she comes to us for counseling, saying, "My husband and I don't agree about this. What should we do?" In 99.9 percent of these situations, the wife just needs to be in submission to God's delegated authority in her life.

My wife chose to give herself to me. She knew what was coming when we got married. She didn't say, "Okay, I will marry you, Robb," and then think, *But I plan on deceiving you about what I'm willing to do in this marriage. The truth is, I'm not going to love you; I'm not going to serve God with you; I'm not going to cook for you; and I'm not going to clean the house. When I'm not out spending your money, I'm going to lie around and put on eight hundred pounds eating chocolate bonbons!*

Linda didn't do that; she has been a faithful, wonderful wife to me in every aspect. But if that had been the case, would I then be expected to just accept it?

This question often arises when a person is married to someone who doesn't listen to God. For instance, you may be thinking, My spouse wants me to walk away from God. Should I do that? No, you have the wrong idea about submission if you think you should submit to that request. You are first called to submit to God. No one ever takes His place in your life except His delegated authority who believes and acts on what He has already said. Let this principle eliminate any confusion you may have.

As a parent, do you think it is right for you to say something to your children and then have them go out and do exactly the opposite of what you just told them? No, that is rebellion.

Well, it is the same thing when it happens in the marriage relationship. For example, it is absolute rebellion for a husband not to love his wife as Jesus loves him.

There are times I may not like what Linda is saying to me; I may not even think that what she is saying is correct. But when she opens her mouth, that is usually the end of every situation because I love her. I am not controlled by her, but I love her.

And because I love my wife, I won't ask her to do something stupid. I will ask her to do only what is within the parameters of the written Word of God because the head of the woman is the man, but the head of the man is Christ. If I ever told her that I wanted her to do something that was illegal or immoral, I wouldn't be able to walk a foot and a half before I'd have Jesus' hand around my throat. He would tell me that my rebellion stinks and that I need to retract what I just said to my wife. Please remember the situation that Abraham encountered in Genesis 20:1-6 with Abimilech. God told Abimilech that if he touched Sarah he was a dead man and so was his nation for that sin against God. God our father can protect us even when our authority walks in fear. Recently as Linda was preparing to travel to another city to minister the Word, she asked me if there was anything I would like her to say. So I wrote out something I wanted her to say while she was there. Linda could have responded that she didn't feel like saying what I wrote out for her, but she didn't because she has a submitted heart.

On the other hand, I could have said that I didn't want to send my wife to that city to speak. How could I do that? It's simple. God's world is not a democracy. The majority does not rule. The guy with the biggest mouth does not rule in God's kingdom.

When God delegates authority to you, you don't have to talk loud. At home, I never need to raise my voice. I just say, "Sorry, we are not going this way. This is what we are going to do. You can jump, scream, shout, run around the house, or do whatever you want, but we are not going this way. That's the way it is."

I don't get high blood pressure. I don't get upset with people. I just submit to my authority, Jesus Christ, and follow His leading in the areas He has given me authority, including my home.

If you are a wife, let me address you for a moment. The Bible says three times in Ephesians 5 that you are to be subject to and reverence your husband. Therefore, the biggest problem in the home arises when you challenge your husband. That challenge will be the greatest challenge he faces all day because he doesn't know what to do with it. What can he do when you challenge him? He can't knock you down. He just wants you to understand.

Do you remember the comedy show *I Love Lucy*? Put your name in there, and you'll find out the truth. Adam started it all with I Love Eve. Think about it. Adam changed his entire life because he loved Eve. Ricky Ricardo always changed his life for Lucy. I've had my own I Love Linda show. At times I've made the mistake of changing direction and not doing what God wanted me to do out of my love for her. I didn't want to hurt her, but I ended up hurting us both.

You see, when you cause your husband to leave the parameters of God's will for his life, you are stretching beyond the boundaries of whom God called him to be in your life. Your husband is to submit upward to his Head, Jesus Christ—not downward to you.

Jesus entrusted Himself to the Father, who "judges justly" (1 Peter 2:23 NIV). When does that principle ever pertain to your life? When you agree with your God-ordained authority? No, because you are not having to use your faith when you agree. You have to entrust yourself to the Father who judges justly when it's time to submit in the midst of disagreement.

When you disagree with your husband, entrust yourself and your family to God. Lean on His promises to you, such as the following scriptures:

> Trust in the LORD, and do good;
> Dwell in the land, and feed on His faithfulness.
> Delight yourself also in the LORD,
> And He shall give you the desires of your heart.
> Commit your way to the LORD,
> Trust also in Him,
> And He shall bring it to pass. (Ps. 37:3–5)

> Trust in the LORD with all your heart,
> And lean not on your own understanding;
> In all your ways acknowledge Him,
> And He shall direct your paths. (Prov. 3:5–6)

God will take care of you. He guarantees it! When you submit yourself to the Word and to the husband He has placed in authority in your home, you give the Holy Spirit free rein to work His will in your home.

CHILDREN'S SUBMISSION TO PARENTS

How does this concept of "submission is not agreement" apply to children? It's simple. The Bible says that as they entrust themselves to Him who judges justly and obey their parents in the Lord, they will live long and things will go well for them on this earth (Eph. 6:1–3).

I wish I could do this part of my life all over again. Then if my dad told me to do something, I would say, "Yes, sir, whatever you say, sir. It doesn't matter to me—whatever you want. What would you like for me to do next?" He'd have to run out of things sooner or later!

I know my dad loves me; he has a soft heart. After a little while, he would start thinking he was picking on me and stop. But he wouldn't stop giving me things to do as long as he sensed any rebellion in me—as long as I was just obedient and not willing.

You may think you are getting your kids to do what you tell them to do. But stay alert to the condition of their hearts. It's possible that they are only obeying you until they get bigger than you!

SUBMISSION IN THE WORKPLACE

What about submission on the job? Ephesians 6:5–7 tells us that we are to give our service to our masters as unto the Lord:

> Bondservants, be obedient to those who are your masters according to the flesh, with fear and trembling, in sincerity of heart, as to Christ; not with eyeservice, as menpleasers, but as bondservants of Christ, doing the will of God from the heart, with goodwill doing service, as to the Lord, and not to men.

How you relate as an employee to your employer is a very big deal to God. For instance, let's consider Joseph's example again. Joseph was taken away from his family and made a slave. He didn't wallow in bitterness and hatred. Instead, when he was mistreated, he responded by forgiving the offender and doing an even better job. Potiphar saw that everything prospered under Joseph's hand, so he made Joseph overseer of his whole house.

That's the kind of employee you need to be. Your employer should recognize that everything prospers under your hand as well. In fact, I'll go so far as to say this: don't expect promotion in life if things don't prosper under your hand.

People think they are supposed to get a raise just because they go to work. They think, *It is the first of the year, so it must be raise time!* But if a person's boss didn't give him a raise the last time he expected it, perhaps the reason is that he didn't give his boss much more than a body to fill a position at the workplace.

I give people who work for me a "talent"—a responsibility or a task to fulfill; then I expect them to multiply what I've given them, and they always do. I have an awesome church staff, and I'm very proud of them.

If someone gives you a responsibility to fulfill at your job, you should make it your goal to go beyond what has been asked of you. Don't have the attitude that you won't do anything unless you get paid for it. If you don't do anything, you won't get paid for it. Prosperity isn't going to bother you when you live in poverty thinking.

Joseph made everything in Potiphar's household prosper. His success even got Potiphar thinking about Joseph's God.

That's a good way to be a witness at work. Cause everything in your sphere of responsibility to prosper, and make your boss look great. Doing that works a lot more effectively than witnessing to coworkers at the workplace while neglecting your work. When you do that, you put your boss in a position of having to ask you to do your job.

Later Joseph's divinely delegated authority jumped off God's track when Potiphar's wife tried to seduce him. Joseph then backed up to his next level of delegated authority, which was God, and said, "How then can I do this great wickedness, and sin against God?" (Gen. 39:9).

Your boss might tell you, "It is all right to steal," or "I want you to lie and cheat for me." If that ever happens, you have to say, "Boss, I esteem you, and I want to be your servant with all my heart. But I can't cheat, Boss. I won't spread around what you just asked of me, but I can't cheat." If you are the boss's best worker, he won't fire you for taking that position. But even if you are fired God will get you a better job. Getting fired for standing up for what is right is only an indicator that you were at the wrong place of employment. Never compromise your position no matter what the cost and you'll be delivered the same way Shadrach, Meshach, and Abed-Nego were delivered. Whenever one of your delegated authorities violates his divinely ordained boundaries, you have to back up to the next level of authority. Of course, you can never opt out of submitting to that position of delegated authority, only to that particular person.

However, as long as your employer stays within God's boundaries, you are to obey what he asks you to do. When he tells you, "I'd like you to do this," it isn't open for discussion; you need to do it!

Don't be obedient because you are being made to be obedient. Be willing as well. Be a vital part of the boss's team. The only way your boss will get to know Jesus through your witness is by watching you and realizing that something is different about you. He may not like what you say sometimes, but he'll know he can always count on you.

SUBMISSION IN THE CHURCH

In the church, you are to obey those who have the rule over you and submit yourself to them. If you don't think you can submit right now with a right attitude, start out by obeying. Obedience can be without willingness, even though that isn't God's best.

Remember, Samuel told Saul that rebellion is witchcraft. It is manipulation and control of a situation in order to get one's own way. Obedience is better than a person's fake worship.

So often people are gung ho when they first start serving God. They come into the church all excited. They are really turned on to God. They come to every service, eager to hear what the pastor has to say.

Then something changes. When the pastor sees them at church, he realizes he isn't looking at them anymore; he's looking at individuals with no resemblance to who they were before. He looks into their eyes and sees suspicion. He watches them distance themselves from him. But these people aren't pulling away from their pastor; they are pulling away from God because rebellion has crept into their lives.

People tell me that my standard for this issue of submission is way too high. But let's put my standard next to God's, and then you'll be able to see whose standard is really high!

Submission Is Ultimately Unto God

I thank God with all my heart that I learned on the front side of my Christian walk (not on the back side) that submission isn't agreement. I can think of many people who were once doing well in their walk with the Lord, but then they opted out because of rebellion. They can come back to the Lord again, but it's always a little harder to completely surrender one's will the second time around.

That's why you should never let rebellion creep in and compromise your walk with the Lord. Don't ever compromise your life for anything.

One of the greatest problems the body of Christ faces today is something I mentioned before: people tend to submit downward instead of upward. Those above them in authority are the ones they are suspicious of; those below them are the ones they believe.

But those below you have only limited knowledge; they are only guessing about what they are saying. Meanwhile, they are in a frantic race to sew one fig leaf on to another as they try to make an apron to cover up their nakedness of rebellion and of the refusal to ultimately submit to God.

Here's another thing about submission I learned early on: submission doesn't have anything to do with another person; it is only between me and God.

Do I trust God enough to be willing to submit to those to whom He has assigned me? Can I trust Him enough to give my heart and joyfully yield who I am to someone else?

If anything ever goes wrong in my submission to my delegated authorities, I must trust God to rescue me and to take care of me. Only therein can I find the security I need. But as long as I refuse in some way to submit—as long as I make submitting an option in my life—God cannot bless me the way He wants to.

Most Christians don't understand how to trust God on this level. Thus, their lives are continually in agitation. They act suspicious of others. They hold tightly to their opinions and refuse to yield to the legitimate authorities in their lives. But Psalm 23:1–2 (KJV) gives them their answer in the midst of their turmoil: "The LORD is my shepherd; I shall not want. He maketh me to lie down in green pastures: he leadeth me beside the still waters."

We already saw that Jesus is our example of how to utterly submit to God. First Peter 2:21, 23 (NIV) illustrates that example:

To this you were called, because Christ suffered for you, leaving you an example, that you should follow in his steps . . . When they hurled their insults at him, he did not retaliate; when he suffered, he made no threats. Instead, he entrusted himself to him who judges justly.

When you read these verses, you may think, *I've really been making mistakes in how I respond to difficult situations with those in authority.* Well, don't keep on making the same mistakes. Stop the cycle of defeat!

Notice again that Jesus "entrusted himself to him who judges justly." Why did Jesus have to do that? Because from the time Jesus woke up in the morning to the time He went to bed at night, He faced injustices. People took advantage of Him. People did things to Him that were wrong. Through it all, He entrusted Himself to Him who judges justly.

Jesus entrusted Himself to God when the Jewish leaders hung Him on a cross. When they said, "We have You now!" He said, "I could call ten legions of angels to help Me."

But Jesus didn't try to defend Himself. Instead, He let the soldiers take Him away. He allowed them to say whatever they wanted to say about Him. It didn't matter because He didn't believe them; He believed God.

Avoid Offense at All Costs

Your relationships with people are always based on your relationship with God. It's not the other way around. Your relationship with God is not based on your relationships with people.

Most people have it backward. They backslide when someone does something that is wrong. They always expect the other person to be the one who first forgives.

I have determined that I will never even think about what others do against me. I don't want to live in offense because I know what it will cost me.

People who continually get offended are people who always see life through their own selfish perspective. Their attitude is "as long as everything is okay with me, this relationship can go on. As long as you don't step on my toes, everything is fine." But watch out if you make a mistake and step on their toes!

I'm not like that. When a person steps on my toes, I forgive him because I am committed. I made a decision about my commitment to that person long before any offense showed up.

Your commitment to your authorities must be well in place before offense has an opportunity to show up. Then when an offense does occur, you will be ready to respond according to God's love—ever ready to believe the best of every person.

But let me give you a clue—you cannot be ever ready to believe the best of every person if you are sitting back with a score card determining whether your authorities are good or bad every time you wake up in the morning. You have to get rid of judgmental thoughts such as, I don't like the way they fixed their hair yesterday. I don't like the way they acted in that situation. I don't think they treated that person right. I know why they said what they just said, etc., etc.

What really matters is that you understand this scriptural principle: the moment you get offended is the moment your spiritual growth stops. Until you rid yourself of all bitterness and resentment and get your heart right in the matter, you can never move any farther toward winning the heart of God. Therefore, let me give you a practical definition of submission. Submission is the willingness to bow my knee before men in order to satisfy the requirements of Heaven.

WILL YOU BE A SAUL OR A DAVID?

Now I want to talk about an important issue that the body of Christ desperately needs to deal with. I'm talking about the issue of transferring submission from the head to the heart.

I can tell when people come to me submitting only from their heads. I know when I have a person's heart or when a person is holding himself at bay from me.

God is looking for people of the heart, not people of the head. He is looking for people who live their lives from within, not from without; people who are not just focused on promoting their self-interests, but are focused on giving their God-ordained authorities full-time servanthood.

Second Chronicles 16:9 (NASB) records, "The eyes of the LORD move to and fro throughout the earth that He may strongly support those whose heart is completely His." God is looking for hearts that hold nothing back from Him.

Jesus confirmed this in John 4:23: "The hour is coming, and now is, when the true worshipers will worship the Father in spirit and truth; for the Father is seeking such to worship Him." God seeks people who worship Him from their hearts in a truthful manner. These people are honest with others as well. They don't speak in half-truths, trying to befriend people just to be able to extract information for their own selfish benefit.

David's greatest counselor, Ahithophel, was a man whose heart held back truth from his king. When Ahithophel betrayed David by siding with Absalom, David wrote this concerning him: "The words of his mouth were smoother than butter, but war was in his heart" (Ps. 55:21). Do you know that Ahithophel killed himself a year later? He saw that what he had done was irreparable. There was no way he could get back to what God had planned for him, so he ended his life.

God always searches for a man whose heart is perfect toward Him. When He looked for a king for Israel, He said that Saul was that type of man. But Saul didn't remain perfect in heart. When Samuel questioned Saul about his disobedience to the Lord's command to destroy everything that was Amalekite, Saul said he kept the best of the livestock and left King Agag alive because the people told him that was what he should do. The people caused Saul to do what God did not want him to do, and as a result, Saul lost it all.

If you're not careful, people will cause you to lose out on what God has planned for your life as well. There is no room inside your heart for people's opinions and your natural reasonings. There is no room for anything other than yielding your life to the Father's will day after day after day. Promotion doesn't come from the east or the west. Promotion comes only from the Lord

(Ps. 75:6–7). As you humble yourself under the mighty hand of God and keep a perfect, submitted heart before Him, He will exalt you in due time.

When Saul and Jonathan were killed in battle, did you ever wonder why David said, "How are the mighty fallen"? Well, I'll tell you why. When David looked at Saul, he didn't see a man who was constantly trying to kill him. David didn't see a man who was so fear driven that he had to have David play his instrument in his presence to get rid of the evil spirits that tormented him. David saw only a man who was the anointed of the Lord. So when David said, "How are the mighty fallen," he was lamenting the day that the Lord's anointed king no longer believed what God said.

As for you, you must choose continually whether you are going to live this life as a "Saul" or as a "David." Saul's heart was tainted with pride and rebellion. In contrast, 1 Samuel 13:14 notes that when God looked for someone to replace Saul whose heart was perfect toward Him, the man He found was David—a man after His own heart.

GOD DESIRES
A POOR AND CONTRITE HEART

Isaiah 66:1–2 tells us the condition of heart that God desires us to have:

> Thus says the LORD:
> "Heaven is My throne,

And earth is My footstool.
Where is the house that you will build Me?
And where is the place of My rest?
For all those things My hand has made,
And all those things exist,"
Says the LORD.
"But on this one will I look:
On him who is poor and of a contrite spirit,
And who trembles at My word."

A "poor" heart doesn't mean a heart that lacks what it needs. It means a helpless heart. It's the kind of heart that understands completely what Jesus meant when He said, "For without Me you can do nothing" (John 15:5).

Jesus wasn't talking about anything you can do on your own. He was talking about something that can only be done spiritually.

For instance, you can wake up tomorrow morning and decide to go to work and make money on your own. Money isn't hard to make; it is a cinch. All you need to do is to learn how a particular financial deal operates. Once you know that, you can make money. Money is elusive, but it isn't hard to make.

But God looks to the person who is completely dependent on Him for what only He can give—to the one who has a poor and contrite spirit. When God's Word is spoken, this person trembles. When God's name is mentioned, he bows his knee within his heart. When he learns what God's Word says, he has no more questions. If God said it, it is true. If He said so, that is the way it is.

The person God is not looking for is the one who sits in the seat of mockery and halfhearted commitment, deciding whether or not he wants to do what God has told him to do. This is the believer to whom God's Word means little or nothing. He always has a "yes, but . . . ," to offer as an excuse for refusing to submit.

- "Yes, but you just don't know what I've gone through."

- "Yes, but you just don't understand me."

- "Yes, but this is my opinion."

God isn't looking for excuses. He's looking for someone who knows that he is nothing and that God is everything in his life.

MARY'S HEART OF SUBMISSION

John 12 relates an account about Mary, the sister of Lazarus, the man whom Jesus raised from the dead. You need to understand a great truth regarding a submitted heart in this account, especially if you've been banging against that invisible "glass ceiling" in your life.

Six days before the Passover, Jesus came to Bethany, where Lazarus was who had been dead, whom He had raised from the dead. There they made Him a supper; and Martha served, but Lazarus was one of those who sat at the table with Him. Then Mary took a pound of very costly oil of spikenard, anointed the feet of Jesus, and wiped His feet

with her hair. And the house was filled with the fragrance
of the oil. (John 12:1–3)

In the parallel accounts of this incident in Matthew 26, Mark
14, and Luke 7, the Bible says that Mary broke open an alabaster
box filled with a costly ointment. Once the box was opened,
it could never be resealed. Yet the contents of this particular
alabaster box were worth an entire year's wages!

Mary wept as she broke open the alabaster box and poured the
costly ointment over the head and feet of Jesus (Luke 7:38).
Then she wiped His feet with her hair. In this humble act of love,
Mary demonstrated the complete yielding of her heart to Jesus.

Here's what you can learn from Mary: when you worship
God, you must not play games. When you submit your heart to
Him, it is serious business. Halfhearted submission is a mockery
of His sacrifice for you.

Whenever we make submission and obedience optional, based
on whether or not we agree, we make a mockery of what God has
commanded us to do. As long as submission is optional, we will
never accomplish anything God wants us to do.

Nothing gets accomplished when agreement becomes the
requirement for obedience because people never totally agree
about anything. No matter what decision a person in authority
makes, there is always someone who wants to disagree with that
decision.

I wish you could sit in my pastor's seat for a while. If you did,
you'd never want to do it again! You'd find out that every time you
say one thing, fifteen hundred people hear it in fifteen hundred

different ways. You get at least eight telephone calls to inform you that you said something wrong.

What is the source of this problem? People are submitting in their heads but not in their hearts. Not only that, but they are basing their false brand of submission on agreement instead of God-ordained authority.

This problem greatly hinders the effect of a church on its community for the kingdom of God. How is a church going to take its city for Jesus if the people in that church can't even decide which Sunday school class is supposed to go to the bathroom at what time?

I am speaking here to the entire body of Christ. This message is for the church at large because we Christians often have a horrible reputation of being dishonest and hypocritical. On one of our good days, we tell people we are Christians. Then these same people look at our lives and hear us arguing with our spouses through the walls when our doors are closed. And yet we say, "We're going to take this city for God!" Until our hearts become completely submitted to God, we're not going to take anything for Him!

Now let's find out what happened when the disciples saw Mary's act of love toward Jesus.

> One of His disciples, Judas Iscariot, Simon's son, who would betray Him, said, "Why was this fragrant oil not sold for three hundred denarii and given to the poor?" This he said, not that he cared for the poor, but because he was a thief, and had the money box; and he used to take what was put in it. (John 12:4–6)

Judas was a thief in the natural sense, but people can be thieves even when they don't necessarily take material goods from others. A person can be a spiritual thief—in other words, someone who covets something another person has. A spiritual thief goes to great lengths to cover up his nakedness, hiding behind the fig leaf with the hidden fine print that says, "Pride" and "Covetousness."

Jesus responded to Judas: "Let her alone; she has kept this for the day of My burial. For the poor you have with you always, but Me you do not have always" (John 12:7–8).

Believers must get over the fact that someone else might have something they don't have. They need to stop judging other people's prosperity as "excess" that should be given to the poor.

Many believers have the unspoken attitude, "People are fine as long as they make a few thousand bucks a year less than I do. Excess is okay as long as I'm the one who has it!" This attitude has hurt the body of Christ, but people often refuse to recognize it in themselves.

Another thing we can learn from Mary is the depth of sorrow she felt in her heart for her past life of sin. This quality of deep repentance is often missing in the church today. Instead, there is a tremendous amount of flippant forgiveness among believers.

It's so easy for us to forgive someone or to ask for forgiveness flippantly when our hearts aren't in it and everything is coming out of our heads. Too often we approach God without any true sorrow over the sins we have committed.

I sit in my office and ask people if they realize what they have done to themselves spiritually because of their sin. They often act as if they don't care because, after all, God forgave them! But they need to care because a casual attitude about disobedience and rebellion will cause only more harm in their lives and in the lives of those around them in the future.

Get this truth deep in your heart: what you do in your life affects other people. Israel bit the dust in their war against the Philistines because of Saul. The nation of Israel was judged over the sin of that one man!

Knowing this, I have fallen on my face before God over the past several years and said, "Judge me, Lord. If there be any wickedness in my heart, judge me. And, Lord, I know that Satan desires to sift as wheat the people I minister to, so I ask You to make sure that their faith does not fail."

When We Fail a Test

You need to do the same thing before the Lord. Submit your heart completely to Him; otherwise, you'll keep failing test after test, and you'll never get close to His heart.

You see, everything that comes to you in life comes as a test of how you will run your race tomorrow. If you pass the test, you give yourself a platform from which you can run your spiritual race with success for the rest of your life.

There have been times when I have seen some mighty people in the Lord fail their tests. Let's look once more at David's biggest failure in order to gain insight into how we should respond if we fail one of our tests.

How did David ever fall into sin with Bathsheba? Well, we know his adultery with Bathsheba didn't all of a sudden happen one night. David's heart must have been out of fellowship with God for a while. How can we know that? Because a person after God's own heart doesn't see a temptation one time and immediately become willing to change his entire life and hurt his fellowship with God by yielding to it.

During the time David's heart was hardening toward the Lord, he saw Bathsheba out on her roof bathing. Over a period of time, he began to dwell on his lust for her, and that lust blinded him to the consequences of adultery.

That doesn't mean David was unaware of what was coming if he yielded to that temptation. You can't tell me a man and a woman don't know that adultery will destroy their lives. David and Bathsheba knew what they were doing.

So David saw Bathsheba bathing on the roof. How long do thoughts of adultery have to work on a person before he yields to them? Between one and two years? I don't know the exact amount of time. I do know that David didn't suddenly decide to commit adultery and then immediately act on that decision. The thoughts of adultery worked on him every day, every day, every day, until he finally became inclined to act on those thoughts.

One day David saw Bathsheba bathing, and his hardened heart caused his resolve to break. "Bring that woman to me," he told his servants.

The Bible says that when David lay with Bathsheba that night, she conceived. Later Bathsheba sent the king a message informing him of the child in her womb. Upon reading her message, David notified Joab to send in Uriah the Hittite, Bathsheba's husband.

Many have the idea that no one else pays for the sin they commit. Uriah certainly paid for David's sin.

Uriah was a faithful husband and soldier in the king's army. David offered him a drink and told him to go lie with his wife as a reward for the good job he had done. But instead, Uriah slept in front of the palace.

When David asked him why he hadn't gone home to his wife, Uriah replied, "As long as the ark of the Lord is housed in a tent and the men you gave me are sleeping on the ground, I will not do that." (See 2 Sam. 11:1.) We must understand two things. First, this was at the time that kings go out to battle and David did not go. Second, Uriah walked in the integrity David did at one time and Uriah's character convicted David. David got Uriah drunk, thinking he could weaken Uriah's resolve and then send in Bathsheba. But his idea didn't work; Uriah wouldn't go anywhere near his wife. (Can you imagine what kind of fight that would create in the home? "Why didn't you want to come home and see me?" the wife would rave. "I haven't seen you for three months, and you don't even want to be around me for a couple of hours!")

You have to think this through. Uriah was a dedicated, self-controlled man. His loyalty and his faithfulness would not permit him to go to her.

David realized he wasn't going to get anywhere with Uriah, so he sent a message back with him to Joab. In effect, David put Uriah's death warrant into the man's own hand. Uriah faithfully delivered the message to Joab—a message that said, "Set Uriah in the heat of the battle; then pull the men back and leave him there so he will be killed by the enemy." (See 2 Sam. 11:15.)

You know, that is exactly the way many people treat each other. When the heat is turned up and the pressure is on, they walk out on the relationship and leave the other person alone to face the storms of life. In God's eyes, the way a person responds to heat is the measure that makes him either a vessel of honor or a vessel of dishonor.

Joab ordered his men to take the battle close to the wall so they could conquer the city. Uriah was up on the front lines, where the men were so close to the city walls that a woman was able to throw a millstone down and kill one of David's valiant and mighty men. Many of David's best men died that day—all because of David's order to Joab to eliminate Uriah.

Then Joab pulled back everyone except Uriah, as the king had ordered. As a result, Uriah was killed. Afterward, Joab wrote a message to David, telling him that his soldiers were getting their brains kicked in and that several of David's valiant men had been killed when they pressed close to the city walls. Joab told the messenger, "When the king becomes irate, tell him that Uriah the Hittite is dead also."

The messenger traveled back to Jerusalem and gave the king Joab's message. Before David could get angry about the bad news, the messenger added that Uriah the Hittite was dead also. Upon hearing that, David calmed down and told the messenger to take back a message of comfort to Joab.

For the rest of Bathsheba's pregnancy, David stayed out of fellowship with God. One day, the Lord sent Nathan the prophet to request an audience with the king. Nathan opened with this statement:

There were two men in one city, one rich and the other poor. The rich man had exceedingly many flocks and herds. But the poor man had nothing, except one little ewe lamb which he had bought and nourished; and it grew up together with him and with his children. It ate of his own food and drank from his own cup and lay in his bosom; and it was like a daughter to him. And a traveler came to the rich man, who refused to take from his own flock and from his own herd to prepare one for the wayfaring man who had come to him; but he took the poor man's lamb and prepared it for the man who had come to him. (2 Sam. 12:1–4)

When David heard this, he said, "Nathan, tell me who this man is, for he should die for what he has done!"

Nathan replied, "You are the man."

Right then, David could have had Nathan killed and kept anyone else from ever knowing what he had done. David could have sewed another fig leaf upon his apron and hidden behind it for the rest of his life.

After all, David was Israel's pastor; he had shepherded them wisely for years. When he became their king, they were being continually hurt, tormented, and killed by the enemies surrounding them. Since then, David had brought peace to his country, and his people were no longer in fear. Once again, the people were beginning to know the ways of God, and God was blessing them for it. Under David's reign, the people and the nation of Israel had flourished.

All these thoughts were probably flying through David's mind.

His natural mind was screaming, *What am I going to do? Should I try to cover this up?*

But David's heart smote him with the conviction of the Holy Spirit, and in the end he chose to follow his heart and not his head. He submitted to the Lord's chastening as he said to Nathan, "I have sinned against the LORD" (2 Sam. 12:13).

> Nathan said to David, "The LORD also has put away your sin; you shall not die. However, because by this deed you have given great occasion to the enemies of the LORD to blaspheme, the child also who is born to you shall surely die." (2 Sam. 12:13–14)

Read that last verse, and then try to tell me that other people don't have to pay for your sin!

David failed that particular test in a big way, but he responded to the Lord's rebuke with a contrite heart of repentance. And although David suffered consequences for his sin for the rest of his life, God still considered him qualified to be called a man after His own heart.

DAVID'S BROKEN AND CONTRITE HEART

After Nathan's confrontation, David voiced his repentance before God:

> O Lord, open thou my lips; and my mouth shall shew forth thy praise. For thou desirest not sacrifice; else would

I give it: thou delightest not in burnt offering. The sacrifices of God are a broken spirit: a broken and a contrite heart, O God, thou wilt not despise. (Ps. 51:15–17 KJV)

God looks for a broken and contrite heart when we fail our tests. That doesn't sound like flippant forgiveness to me!

Young's Literal Translation says it this way in verse 17: "A heart that is broken and bruised you will not despise." The Basic English Bible has "a broken and sorrowing heart." The Bible in Living English puts it this way: "A heart that is broken and battered down you will not despise." The Living Bible states, "It is a broken spirit you want—remorse and penitence."

The Message provides an interesting paraphrase of these verses:

> Unbutton my lips, dear God;
> I'll let loose with your praise.
> Going through the motions doesn't please you,
>   a flawless performance is nothing to you.
> I learned God-worship
>   when my pride was shattered.
> Heart-shattered lives ready for love
>   don't for a moment escape God's notice.

This psalm shows us the importance of true heart repentance when we fail the test. It also shows us the reason we often don't feel forgiven: we don't let our sin touch our hearts the way it touches the One we sin against.

WAIT ON THE LORD

Even after David's life was broken—even after he had missed it and betrayed God—the desire of his heart was to spend precious time in God's presence. In Psalm 27:3–4, David talked about this:

> Though an army may encamp against me,
> My heart shall not fear;
> Though war may rise against me,
> In this I will be confident.
> One thing I have desired of the LORD,
> That will I seek:
> That I may dwell in the house of the LORD
> All the days of my life,
> To behold the beauty of the LORD,
> And to inquire in His temple.

Beholding God's beauty doesn't mean you glance at Him once and then look away. When you behold something, you gaze at it. When you behold the beauty of the Lord, you see Jesus and all that He is. You let Him touch your life as you bask in His presence.

David went on to say in verse 13:

> I would have lost heart, unless I had believed
> That I would see the goodness of the LORD
> In the land of the living.

Then he gave us good advice for our hard times when we have to face our failures before God:

> Wait on the LORD;
> Be of good courage,
> And He shall strengthen your heart;
> Wait, I say, on the LORD! (v. 14)

In other words, shut your ears and your mouth to everything except God and His love that never fails!

I want to say one more thing about submission. There are thousands of ways to please God, but not one of them is without faith. Faith is the substance of things hoped for. If you don't see something in your authority's life that you want to see, pray for him. No one is perfect, but that doesn't change the fact that you must submit to that person's authority in your life.

If you don't like something the authority says or does, take it up with God because He is the One who has commanded you to keep a submitted heart. And if you don't particularly like the person in authority over you, take that up with God too. He made that person the same way He made you!

Above all, give up your will to God. Go for the greatest thing you can live for—winning the Father's heart. Whether you live another fifty, sixty, or seventy years, that is really a short time in light of eternity. Then you'll be out of here, and everything about you will be history. Choose obedience and submission every day of your life. Let it be said of you by those you leave behind: "He [or she] was truly a person after God's own heart."

Part 2:

A LOYAL HEART

Chapter 6

THE FOUNDATION OF FAITHFULNESS

We must have an anchor we can count on, a solid foundation upon which we can build our lives. Otherwise, all we're doing is "playing crawdads" in the bucket of life.

When a bunch of crawdads are dumped into a bucket together, they start crawling all over each other, doing everything they can to get out of that bucket. But those crawdads aren't working together to achieve their goal. Inside that bucket, it's every crawdad for himself!

You'd think that the crawdad on the top of the pile would be the most likely to win. But just as that lucky crawdad reaches out with his claws to grab onto the bucket rim, pull himself up, and climb out, the crawdads under him all fall down on purpose.

You see, no self-respecting crawdad will ever let another crawdad get out of that bucket before he does. Each one is trying to use the other crawdads to get himself to the top of the bucket where he can jump over the rim.

Some people act just like those crawdads in the bucket all the time. The guy on top of the pile is always scrambling to grab onto anything that will take him "over the bucket rim" into fame, fortune, and success. At the same time, those below him are doing all they can to keep him from getting to that bucket rim before they do.

BUILDING A LIFE OF VIRTUE

Why is this kind of behavior so rampant among us? Because we live in a society that is increasingly defined by a breakdown of virtues. We're not even sure what the word virtue means anymore!

Many people's understanding of basic virtues has degenerated so much that situational ethics now represent the truth to them. Even within the body of Christ, more divorces occur than ever before, and more abortions are performed than ever before. The truth is, there really isn't much difference between the world and the church in regard to foundational virtues. Even in the pulpit, ministers are often confused about what virtue really is.

What is our role as we live in the midst of this breakdown in virtue? What can cause us to move beyond self-centeredness and become a cool drink for others in the desert of this unkind life?

The answer is simple: we must become people of virtue. We must build a life of virtue on the same foundation as our virtuous God.

We find this principle in 2 Peter 1:3–4:

As His divine power has given to us all things that pertain to life and godliness, through the knowledge of Him who called us by glory and virtue, by which have been given to us exceedingly great and precious promises, that through these you may be partakers of the divine nature, having escaped the corruption that is in the world through lust.

"Lust" in verse 4 isn't necessarily referring to physical desire or sensual pressure. This verse is saying that by the power of God's promises, we will actually escape an unsound, virtueless society and become virtuous. Why is this possible? Because God is virtuous.

"Virtue" in this passage also denotes lovingkindness, goodness, and faithful love. God has given us His faithful love, His goodness, and His lovingkindness. His lovingkindness says to us, "I am now giving unto you very great and exceedingly precious promises so that, by these promises, you may become a partaker of My divine nature."

But as I look across the body of Christ, I don't see a tremendous demonstration of God's nature. As a matter of fact, what I've seen more than anything else over the years is a tremendous number of people who take advantage of one another, backbite one another, and use one another for their own selfish purposes. And if anyone has the courage to look these people in the eye and say, "No, you're not going to do that to me anymore," they reply, "Humph! You're a Christian, so you're supposed to forgive!"

If you want to become a person after God's heart, you must become a partaker of His nature. That's why I want to talk to you about how to build a life of virtue. This spiritual process is essential to winning the heart of God.

First, let's talk about the foundation of your "building," which is the same foundation upon which God has based His glory and virtue. I'm talking about the foundation of faithfulness.

Unfaithfulness is growing at an alarming rate in today's society. But in the midst of this epidemic of unfaithfulness, God never ceases to show His faithfulness to us. He is ever faithful to perform His promises on our behalf as we trust in Him.

What Is Faithfulness?

Just what is faithfulness? The word faithful means "constant" and "reliable" and implies "continued, steadfast adherence to a person or thing to which one is bound by an oath, by duty, or by obligation." That obligation is a self-obligation. In other words, I steadfastly perform certain responsibilities in a particular arena because I personally feel obliged to do so. I have a duty to do so. However, that obligation isn't motivated by guilt or external manipulation. No one is controlling me or making me feel obligated.

You see, faithfulness is never a product of control or manipulation. A person who steadfastly performs certain responsibilities out of a sense of guilt is not being faithful; he's being manipulated.

It is possible for a person's spirit to control you so much that it mars your life, changes the countenance on your face, and even speaks through you. If what I just described sounds like your life, you need to admit that you have an ungodly soul tie with someone that needs to be broken. If you don't break that control over your life, you will begin to treat everyone else in your life the same way you've been treated—with manipulation and control, or what you once called faithfulness.

Faithfulness should never be confused with the subject of loyalty. You see, loyalty is a two-way street; it is a quality within a relationship possessed by all parties involved. On the other hand, faithfulness is an inner virtue that a person possesses, regardless of outside circumstances or other people's actions.

Remember this: faithfulness is only the threshold to loyalty. Before you can ever be loyal, you must first be faithful. So don't try to be loyal before you perfect faithfulness. If you will first learn to be faithful, you will avoid much of the disappointment that people experience in their relationships.

GOD IS A FAITHFUL GOD

In learning how to be faithful, you must understand that God Himself is faithful. Deuteronomy 7:9 calls God "the faithful God." Then 1 Corinthians 10:13 gives us this promise regarding God's faithfulness:

> No temptation has overtaken you except such as is common to man; but God is faithful, who will not allow you to be tempted beyond what you are able, but with the temptation will also make the way of escape, that you may be able to bear it.

Think how many times you have heard someone say, "I just can't take it anymore! I just can't! God said He would give me only what I could bear. But I can't bear this!"

What is that person actually saying to God? "God, You're like me. You don't always keep Your word because You have given me more than I am able to bear."

The writer of Hebrews urged, "Let us hold fast the confession of our hope without wavering, for He who promised is faithful" (10:23). God is consistent. He is reliable. He is bound by His oath to us. He has a covenant obligation to us that He has imposed upon Himself.

IT IS REQUIRED OF US TO BE FAITHFUL

Not only that, but God requires faithfulness from us: "Moreover it is required in stewards that one be found faithful" (1 Cor. 4:2). To be people after God's own heart, we must become faithful, reliable, and consistent stewards of His truth and partakers of His nature.

When people leave my church and then return years later, they often say, "You know what, Pastor Robb? There is one thing about you—you're consistent!" They think that's a real compliment. But when I hear that, I think, *Well, wait a minute. I haven't even gotten started yet if that's all I am.* If I weren't consistent, I'd be in big trouble because it's required of me to be faithful!

God requires me to be faithful first to Him. I cannot be faithful to you unless I can be faithful to the One I see in you.

Your relationship with every person in your life is first a relationship based on faithfulness to God. When you act on what He has already spoken in His Word, you are acting out of faithfulness to God, even if that action is directed toward another person.

For instance, Jesus said, "Whoever compels you to go one mile, go with him two" (Matt. 5:41). You see, a Roman soldier could pick out a Jew on the street and make him carry his pack for one mile. But Jesus was saying, "Don't just take his pack one mile as the Roman law requires; go the extra mile to help him!" The person who consistently obeyed this command to willingly help out an enemy was showing faithfulness to God.

It is required of all of us to be found faithful, especially in the forgiveness arena. People often come to me and say things like, "Well, I've forgiven that person, and that's all just fine. But, Pastor, you just don't know what he did to me."

I reply, "Let me help you. You haven't really forgiven him."

"Yes, I have!"

"No, you haven't. If you truly forgave him, why is there still a sting? The fact is, there is an open wound that hasn't yet been healed. And I'll tell you what that open wound is called. Its called unforgiveness. Its called undealt-with bitterness. It's called unresolved conflict. Its called unfulfilled vengeance. Please understand you will never forget what has happened between you, the devil will make sure of that. But we must be willing to let go of that pain. One time Jesus' disciple Peter thought he'd get this whole issue of forgiveness straightened out. He said, "I'm going to find out right now from Jesus how much He wants us to forgive."

Jesus had just told His followers how to deal with problems in the church. He said, "Listen, if your brother offends you, go to him. If your brother won't hear you, take with you one or two witnesses. If he still won't hear you, take it to the church." (See Matt. 18:15–17.)

Then Peter asked Jesus, "Lord, how often shall my brother sin against me, and I forgive him? Up to seven times?" (v. 21).

Peter thought he'd go way out there and give an extreme example so Jesus could reply, "No, seven times is too many." But Jesus didn't say that. He said, "No, Peter, I'm not saying you should forgive a person up to seven times or even seventy times. I'm saying you should forgive him up to seventy times seven!"

Immediately the disciples cried, "Oh, Lord, increase our faith!"

Do you know why they said that? Because no matter what God tells us to do, it takes faith to do it. If it doesn't take faith—if it doesn't require us to change and grow in order to be faithful in carrying out that command—then God probably didn't tell us to do it.

Learning to forgive and live free from offense is a vital part of faithfulness. What happens if we don't go through this learning process? When things get a little rough, we begin to justify ourselves, and then we exit from conflict. As a result, there is no resolution to the conflict. Bitterness and unforgiveness build up on the inside. More strife and destruction come—all because we've been taught by the world to pull out instead of forgive when offense occurs.

That's why Christians say, "Sure, I've forgiven them. Hallelujah! They can sit over on that side of the church, and I'll sit over here. That's just fine." Having adopted that attitude, they live for years with unresolved conflict in their hearts, letting it eat away at them on the inside as they shout hallelujah on the outside. These Christians have failed the most fundamental test of their spiritual walk, for they have been found unfaithful in their responsibility to walk in love and forgiveness.

FAITHFULNESS IN MARRIAGE

God's requirement that we faithfully walk in love and forgiveness especially applies to the marriage relationship. In 1 Corinthians 7:10–16 Paul talked about faithfulness in marriage:

> Now to the married I command, yet not I but the Lord: A wife is not to depart from her husband. But even if she does depart, let her remain unmarried or be reconciled to her husband. And a husband is not to divorce his wife. But to the rest I, not the Lord, say: If any brother has a wife who does not believe, and she is willing to live with him, let him not divorce her. And a woman who has a husband who does not believe, if he is willing to live with her, let her not divorce him. For the unbelieving husband is sanctified by the wife, and the unbelieving wife is sanctified by the husband; otherwise your children would be unclean, but now they are holy. But if the unbeliever departs, let him depart; a brother or a sister is not under bondage in such cases. But God has called us to peace. For how do you know, O wife, whether you will save your husband? Or how do you know, O husband, whether you will save your wife?

Romans 12:18 also gives husbands and wives a good guideline to follow in their marriages: "If it is possible, as much as depends on you, live peaceably with all men."

Yet with all this wise counsel from the Lord, Christians are still dumping their marriages at an alarmingly high percentage rate.

"But what can I do to change the situation in my marriage?" you may ask. As much as depends on you, live peaceably with your spouse. Never walk out of your faithfulness to your marriage. Never raise your voice in anger or your hand to strike the one you love. Never walk out of love or in unforgiveness with the person you chose to spend your life with.

However, if your spouse is an unbeliever and chooses to depart, let him or her go. In that case, you have been released from your duty and obligation to that relationship. Your faithfulness and reliability to preserve the marriage are no longer necessary.

BE A FAITHFUL SOWER OF GOOD THINGS

Why would God make faithfulness an absolute requirement of serving Him? Because there is a universal law that is always in operation and can never be denied: the law of sowing and reaping. Ephesians 6:8 describes this unchanging law: "Knowing that whatever good anyone does, he will receive the same from the Lord, whether he is a slave or free."

As you faithfully sow good things into other people's lives, you will receive good in your relationship with the Lord. You need to understand, though, that the law of sowing and reaping is not the law of trading.

You see, most people don't really sow; they trade. They love those who love them. They give to those who give to them. Everything is a trade, even in the marriage relationship.

Don't say you're being faithful to sow acts of love into your marriage if, in fact, it bothers you when you don't get the same thing back from your spouse. In that case, you didn't sow it; you were trading for it. You were trying to buy acts of love directed toward yourself.

Sowing and trading are two different things. Don't ever give yourself the luxury of believing that you're sowing something when you expect to receive something from the person into whose life you have sown. You're not sowing until you have let go of all expectation that you will receive something in return. As you faithfully sow good into people's lives according to God's Word, the day will come when God's promise in Psalm 126:5 will be fulfilled in your life: "Those who sow in tears shall reap in joy."

God Rewards Faithfulness

Not only does God require faithfulness; He also rewards faithfulness.

We can see this principle in the familiar passage in Matthew 25, where Jesus talked about the Great White Throne Judgment. Every person ever born will come before Jesus, and He will put the "goats" on the left and the "sheep"—His faithful ones—on the right. And to the faithful stewards of His truth, He will say, "Well done, good and faithful servant: thou hast been faithful over a few things, I will make thee ruler over many things: enter thou into the joy of thy lord" (Matt. 25:23 KJV).

God rewards faithfulness. Of course, faithfulness also has a great price attached to it. Often the price is rejection. Sometimes the price of faithfulness is enduring misunderstanding or having bad words spoken over you. But I guarantee you this: the prize is always greater than the price!

How does God reward faithfulness? For one thing, He rewards by causing men to promote those who exhibit this foundational virtue.

I'm the kind of person who opens myself up to people immediately. But many times people get the wrong idea about my friendliness. They see it as a stamp of approval on their credibility.

Now, that's not so much their fault as it is mine. As a minister, I need to convey that faithfulness must always be proven before promotion can arrive in one's life.

Too often people want to be promoted before they've been proven faithful. They think they deserve promotion before they have demonstrated that they are consistent and reliable to perform their given responsibilities.

For instance, see if this sounds familiar: "You know, I get ten sick days a year at my job, and I'm going to use them, whether I'm sick or not. My boss can call them 'sick days' if he wants to, but I'm going to call them 'well days.' I've got those days coming to me, so I'm taking them!"

That's a good example of unfaithfulness! An unfaithful person is unreliable and inconsistent. You can't count on him to do what he is supposed to do.

According to Proverbs 20:6, an unfaithful person is a lot easier to find than a faithful one:

> Most men will proclaim each his own goodness,
> But who can find a faithful man?

Why would God say that? Because faithful people are few and very far between.

Almost everyone will tell you that he is faithful. Every person will tell you that he has the goods. But what happens when that person hears something negative about you? Does it cause him to lose respect and esteem for you? Or does it cause him to come to you and say, "Forgive me; I listened to words that caused me to be anything but faithful to you in my heart"? Now, those are the words of a faithful person.

You see, faithfulness has nothing to do with the person you're being faithful to. It isn't dependent on anyone else. Faithfulness is a virtue you must possess within yourself, independent of what anyone else does or does not do.

In Luke 16:10–12, Jesus talked about the absolute importance of proving oneself faithful in the little things before God can trust you with greater things, especially His heart:

> He who is faithful in what is least is faithful also in much; and he who is unjust in what is least is unjust also in much. Therefore if you have not been faithful in the unrighteous mammon, who will commit to your trust the true riches? And if you have not been faithful in what is another man's, who will give you what is your own?

You'll never have your own possessions, anointing, ministry, and so forth until you are first found faithful over what belongs to another man.

Paul echoed this principle: "The things that you have heard from me among many witnesses, commit these to faithful men who will be able to teach others also" (2 Tim. 2:2). "Commit these to faithful men." Before people were mentored, they were proven faithful first—independently of their relationship with their spiritual leader. They had earned a good reputation of being faithful with other people before they were ever entrusted with God's holy things. They were reliable. They could be counted on. They had bound themselves by an oath of duty. They were determined to fulfill their inner obligations. And they were rewarded when their spiritual leaders promoted them into positions of increased responsibility.

Get ready to be tested, my friend, for God will test you to see whether you will be proven faithful or unfaithful—a person who adds value to other people's lives, or one who takes value away. You'll never be remembered for what you've taken out of any relationship. You'll be remembered only for the good that you've deposited into other people's lives.

My hope is that I can deposit in you this day a greater desire to build a life of virtue on the foundation of God's everlasting faithfulness. There is actually no other way to reach your chosen destination, for only as you prove yourself faithful can you understand loyalty and thus take the next step toward winning the heart of God.

Chapter 7

THE STEADFAST LOYALTY OF OUR GOD

In the days when Jehoshaphat was king of Judah, God's people were about to be invaded by the Ammonites and the Moabites. The strength of these two enemy armies combined meant almost certain defeat for the people of Judah.

But Jehoshaphat was a godly king who feared the Lord, and he knew where to seek help—the faithful, covenant-keeping God of Judah. So the king proclaimed a fast throughout all of Judah, and the people gathered together to call upon God to save them.

Standing before the people, Jehoshaphat began to talk to God about the covenant He had made with Israel. The king reminded God of everything He had ever done for His people. In essence, Jehoshaphat was crying out for God's mercy, saying, "God, this is who You are. We need You to be the same Deliverer today that You have been for us in the past!"

Then a prophet of God spoke forth the word of the Lord: "Jehoshaphat! Thus says the LORD to you: 'Do not be afraid nor dismayed because of this great multitude, for the battle is not yours, but God's'" (2 Chron. 20:15). Jehoshaphat had received his answer from heaven, and he knew what to do. His people wouldn't run, and they wouldn't give up. They would "stand still and see the salvation of the LORD" (v. 17).

Jehoshaphat sent out the singers and the priests in white robes to go before the soldiers to the battlefield. They sang, "Praise the Lord, for His lovingkindness and His mercy endure forever! His covenant is to all generations. Praise the Lord!" And by the time they reached the battlefield, the Lord had already taken care of the situation. The two enemy armies had destroyed each other, and there was no one left to fight!

When the Problem Is Bigger Than You Are

You may not realize it, but every day you're continually using your faith to overcome attacks that come against you. However, sometimes an attack comes that is not in the category of the one Jehoshaphat faced. It's the type of problem that plagues and torments your mind because you know you can't beat it with your level of faith.

These are the times you must call on Someone greater than yourself to perform the covenant He has made with you: "Lord, I can't beat fear! It's stronger than I am. I can't beat cancer. I can't beat heart trouble. I can't beat divorce. I can't beat hatred. The only thing I can do is cry out for Your mercy."

That's when God says, "The battle is not yours, but Mine. Stand and see the salvation of the Lord!"

So when you face a problem that is greater than you are, don't take any action that is outside the covenant Jesus purchased for you, for your loyal God will always be there for you.

That's one of the most important truths you can ever grasp: God is loyal. God is faithful. God is always there. He'll never give up on you. He'll never throw in the towel. He'll never give in. He always has you on His mind. In fact, God has your picture in His wallet today! He actually thinks about you all the time, attempting to find ways in which He can show His love to you and perform His covenant on your behalf.

It's such a comfort to know that God's loyalty toward us will never come to an end. Throughout the Bible, we are reminded that His mercies are everlasting. For instance, in Lamentations 3, Jeremiah said,

> Through the LORD's mercies we are not consumed,
> Because His compassions fail not.
> They are new every morning;
> Great is Your faithfulness. (vv. 22–23)

God's mercies and His loyal love toward us are new every morning. But the truth is, it is very difficult for us to fully understand God's faithfulness, loyalty, lovingkindness, and tender mercies. How do we define what is actually the very fiber of who the almighty God is? His loyal love is what makes Him God! It is the energy plant that causes God to become to us who He is in reality—not who we think He is.

A gentleman recently stated to me: "Perception is reality." Well, that's only half true. Perception is reality to the person who is perceiving. But perception is not necessarily reality in God's eyes.

However, it is true that life is a series of perceptions. That's why our perceptions must be brought to the table of truth and dissected with the sword of God's Word:

> For the word of God is living and powerful, and sharper than any two-edged sword, piercing even to the division of soul and spirit, and of joints and marrow, and is a discerner of the thoughts and intents of the heart. (Heb. 4:12)

God's Word is a discerner of thoughts. It is the "umpire" that decides the difference between perception and reality. Therefore, we must go to the Word to learn more about the merciful and loyal nature of our God.

Our Unbreakable Covenant with God

God's covenant love toward us is the kind of love that pursues us all the way until the end. God is not faithful one day and faithless the next. His loyalty toward us never changes. James 1:17 (KJV) promises us that, with God, there "is no variableness, neither shadow of turning."

God's loyal love toward you is a love you can never shake off. He will stand by you in any circumstance you face, no matter what. His love for you is so great that He was willing to send His Son, Jesus Christ, to die for you. Through the death, burial, and resurrection of His Son, God made a blood covenant with you, thus ensuring that He could continually demonstrate His lovingkindness toward you for eternity.

Through that blood covenant, we are bound to God at all times. This covenant is not just a matter of friendship—at least not according to the way friendship is defined in modern society. Today friend is a word that is thrown about in a loose and casual way as if it means nothing. Not too much is demanded of a person we call a friend. One day someone we call a friend might be very nice to us; the next day he might "stab us in the back."

But in Old Testament times, the word friend was never used until a blood covenant was made between two people, and it was used only as a term of honor. It meant something profound to be someone's friend back then. It wasn't just a word that didn't mean anything. A blood covenant was a ritual by which two people bound themselves together until death. Before a covenant was made, there was always an opportunity for someone to bow out or give up on the relationship. There was always an opportunity for unfaithfulness. But once that blood covenant was made, it could not be broken.

That's where the old saying came from that says, "Blood is thicker than water." That saying originated among the Middle Eastern people, but they said it this way: "Blood is thicker than milk." That is, those who made a covenant together remained more faithful to each other than those who sucked the same mother's breast at birth. Why? Because blood had been shed. Blood covenant friends were bound to each other for life. The covenant could not be broken.

In the same way, God's blood covenant with you through Jesus is a covenant that cannot be broken. Jesus spilled His blood to make that covenant; therefore, God cannot and will not break the covenant He has with you that was made possible through the blood of His Son.

It's funny to me when I hear people say that someone can be saved one day, and the next day he can be going to hell on a freight train because of something he did. I walk away thinking, No, that isn't right. God cannot break His covenant with me because He promises in His Word that He will never do that!

I have Jesus' word on it. Jesus said, "No longer do I call you servants, for a servant does not know what his master is doing; but I have called you friends, for all things that I heard from My Father I have made known to you" (John 15:15).

Remember, Jesus spoke this to disciples who understood the meaning of covenant. They knew that a person never called someone a friend until a blood covenant was made between them. Jesus was about to go to the cross, so He was saying to His disciples and to us, "I don't call you servants any longer; I now call you My friends. I make My covenant of lovingkindness and tender mercies with you. It is a covenant purchased by My blood, and it cannot be broken."

"But what if I stumble and sin against God?" you may ask. "Doesn't that affect my covenant with Him?"

Understand this: once you are in covenant with almighty God, Creator of the universe, your performance is not on trial any longer. You may miss it; you may step out of the boundaries of His Word. But your poor performance doesn't break the covenant because the only thing on trial now is the strength of the One who has made covenant with you.

And this doesn't apply only to you as an individual. According to covenant loyalty, kindness shown toward the blood brother was a requirement, even if it cost a person his life. This kindness had to be shown not only between the two who actually made the covenant, but to their children and their children's children as well.

In the same way, God's faithfulness is directed not only toward us, but also to our children and to our children's children. Throughout all our generations, God's faithfulness will remain with our descendants forever.

EXPECTATION #1 IN A BLOOD COVENANT

When you are in a covenant love relationship with another person, you must always remember three expectations. First, you expect that you will always be there for the other person. You won't be there for him only when he is at the end of his rope. You'll be there for him all the time so you can stop him from ever reaching the end of his rope!

Many Christians have no idea what it means to be in a covenant friendship with another believer. For instance, I remember the time a gentleman sat across my desk from me and said, "The only reason I wanted a relationship with you, Pastor Robb, was that I knew it would be good for me."

That man's words could have hurt or offended me. But I replied, "I choose not to hear what you're saying, Brother. Tell me, how can I help you right now?" You see, it didn't matter if that man violated our covenant friendship. What mattered was that I remained faithful to it. Why? Because my number one expectation in that covenant relationship was what I expected of myself.

I already know my flesh. I already know that my first inclination when things get uncomfortable is to run now and make up some kind of spiritual excuse about why I ran later! Since I know that about myself, I must maintain an expectation that even if my covenant commitment takes me to the point of death, it must hold. This is one thing I've learned the hard way after several times of eating the fruit of failure!

You can apply this principle to the employee-employer relationship, to your marriage, and to your relationship with your children. In fact, it applies to any situation where you must interact with other people.

Too many people live shallow lives because they think they have to live by performance. Therefore, they're always competing with the people with whom they have relationships.

For instance, if you and your spouse think you have to live by performance in your home, you are probably telling each other constantly, "You always do this wrong," or "You never do this right." Peace reigns in the home only when each adjusts behavior to the other's whims.

But wait a minute. Unless you establish a sense of security in the marriage relationship—unless each knows he or she is accepted unconditionally by the other spouse—there will never be a platform from which true intimacy and closeness can grow.

Instead, you'll reach a point in your relationship where you always feel paranoid about making a mistake.

There are thirty-two ministries within the church I pastor, and all of them have to go down one funnel that leads to me. However, one thing I require of the people who work with me in the ministry is that they don't walk on eggshells with me. Why? If a leader is always causing the people under his authority to walk on eggshells, nothing gets fixed. If something goes wrong, people think, Oh, no, what if he finds out? and then try to hide the problem.

But since I'm going to find out about the problem sooner or later, I want my staff members to tell me sooner before it gets bigger. After all, I'm utterly committed to helping them fix the situation, whatever it is.

I'll tell you what—if you become a covenant part of the Thompsons' lives, we're going to fight to keep you there. It takes a lot for you to get to that place, but once you get there, bless God, don't walk on eggshells! We're committed to you, so feel free to be yourself, imperfections and all.

You see, when you're committed to someone, you don't require him to be perfect. God certainly doesn't require that of you. He already realizes how you are. He understands that if it wasn't for Him, you'd be going to hell. He knows He is your only hope of saving you from yourself!

Expectation #2 in a Blood Covenant

The second expectation in a covenant love relationship is this: you expect that the other person has an expectation to always be there for you. You don't expect him to always be there for you; he expects it of himself.

I don't ever want to have to go to a person and say, "You know, you really need to be there for me right now because we have a covenant relationship." Then that person would probably start walking around saying, "Oh, man, I made a covenant with Pastor Robb, so I have to do this. I don't want to, but I have to."

No, that isn't the way it's supposed to be! In my covenant relationships, I'm not trying to find my way out of covenant; I'm looking for a way into it. I'm looking for a way I can do something for my covenant friend. I'm looking for a way to answer a problem for him. It's not just a duty; it's a privilege.

Here's another point: the covenant relationships I have in my life depend on me, not on someone else. For instance, my marriage to Linda is a covenant. It matters not to me what Linda says. It matters not what she does. I'm in a covenant with her, and I'm bound to her because of my covenant commitment, not because of what she says or does.

It's the same way with God and His covenant with us. When God could find no one greater to swear by, He swore by Himself to keep the covenant He had made with Abraham and his descendants (Heb. 6:13). I follow Jesus' admonition to swear not by heaven, by earth, or by my own head (Matt. 5:34–37). Instead, I let my "yes" be "yes" in my covenant relationships. As far as I am concerned, once I make a covenant, it will not be broken.

My covenants are based on my integrity, not on anyone else's integrity. The other person's covenant is based on his integrity, not mine. This understanding keeps me from demanding that the other covenant partner perform his part of the covenant. I concentrate on my responsibility to be faithful to my commitment to him.

Being in blood covenant with someone is almost like running a relay race. Yet most people look around for their covenant friend and say, "I wonder if he's going to be there when it's time to pass the baton?" They just aren't sure of that person's loyalty to the covenant. However, when a person is in covenant with God, he can run his relay race as fast as he can, knowing that when it's time to pass the baton, God's hand will be there to receive it!

As you draw closer to God and get to know His heart, you come to the place where you realize He will always be there for you. You don't need to be afraid anymore. Your covenant with Him isn't based on you; it is based on Him, and He is an everlastingly loyal God.

THE FALSE BALANCE

So the first expectation in a blood covenant is that I believe and expect from myself that I will do what I said I would do. Second, I expect that you expect from yourself that you will do what you said you would do.

One problem that often arises in a covenant is that one person keeps the covenant and the other does not. This creates a false balance that destroys trust within a covenant relationship.

That's why we write contracts for everything. We're not really sure whether the person intends to keep the contract, so we write contracts as an attempt to keep the person true to his commitment and to give ourselves a way out just in case things don't work the way we want them to. This seems to be no big deal to us only because it's such a common practice in our society today. But entering into a contract with another party is completely different from making a covenant with that person, where the expectation for faithfulness begins first with us.

The truth is, most of the business conducted in this world today is perverted by this lack of covenant expectation. Second Timothy 3 graphically describes the breakdown of virtue that has led to this epidemic of false balances in our modern society:

> Understand this, that in the last days will come (set in) perilous times of great stress and trouble hard to deal with and hard to bear. For people will be lovers of self and [utterly] self-centered, lovers of money and aroused by an inordinate [greedy] desire for wealth, proud and arrogant and contemptuous boasters. They will be abusive (blasphemous, scoffing), disobedient to parents, ungrateful, unholy and profane. [They will be] without natural [human] affection (callous and inhuman), relentless (admitting of no truce or appeasement); [they will be] slanderers (false accusers, troublemakers), intemperate and loose in morals and conduct, uncontrolled and fierce, haters of good. (vv. 1–3 AMPLIFIED)

Isn't it interesting that so many people don't care about other people today? They don't care what someone else may be going through. Why should I care? they think. As long as I am not the one going through it! That's why so many people try to find ways out of contracts they have entered into. They have lost all sense of covenant loyalty.

EXPECTATION #3 IN A BLOOD COVENANT

Let's look at the third expectation in a covenant relationship. This third expectation is the most difficult to accept in many ways. We must be willing to grow up in order to use it correctly.

The third expectation is that I expect that you will do what you said to me that you would do, and you expect the same from me. The first expectation was my expectation directed toward myself. The second was your expectation directed toward yourself. This third expectation is my expectation directed toward you and yours toward me.

The problem is that we often want to give up the first two expectations and concentrate on this third one. We don't want to expect anything from ourselves; we don't want to make ourselves stay true to our own words of commitment. We want to go past the first expectation and immediately leap to this third one: "I expect that you'll do what you said you would do, even if I don't."

But you can't expect more from the other person in covenant than you do from yourself. That is a false balance and an abomination to the Lord. And I guarantee you this: if you maintain that false balance, you will eventually reap what you have sown.

The truth is, the loyalty demanded by this third expectation will occur in only a very small number of your relationships throughout your entire life. Rarely will you be so confident in your relationship with a person that you will be able to stand before him and say, "I'm putting a demand on my covenant with you. I expect you to fully carry out everything you have committed yourself to."

Very few people ever understand this level of a covenant relationship. Instead, they make big problems for themselves because they try to make demands on people with whom they have no covenant. Thus, they go through life from disappointment to disappointment, continually suspicious of everyone around them. They don't understand that they're trying to gain the right thing from the wrong kind of relationships.

Loyalty to each other demands three things: number one, I'm going to be faithful to you, no matter what; and number two, you're going to be faithful to me, no matter what. I demand of myself that I will be faithful, and you demand of yourself that you will be faithful. You don't have anything to do with my faithfulness, and I don't have anything to do with your faithfulness. But as we fulfill these first two covenant demands, the time will come when we can be confident enough to place the third demand on the covenant—expecting the other to be absolutely loyal and to come through for us whenever a need arises.

Jonah's Experience
with the Loyalty of God

Jonah learned a lesson in loyalty after God commanded him to preach repentance to the city of Nineveh.

Most people have the idea that Jonah was running away from

the call of God on his life. But Jonah wasn't running away from God's call. He was running away because he didn't want to lose face before a despised enemy of Israel.

Here's what Jonah was saying: "God, You told me, 'Go to Nineveh and tell the people there that My judgment is coming.' But I'm not going, Lord, because I know You. I know You keep covenant. I know You're a God who forgives. If I do what You're asking me to do, You're going to end up forgiving those sinners, so there is no way in the world I am going to Nineveh!"

Jonah got on a ship and went out to sea. When a huge storm arose, threatening to sink the ship, Jonah told the crew members that he was their problem and that they should throw him overboard. When the men finally did that, the sea immediately became calm.

But God had already sent a taxi for Jonah in the form of a big fish to pick him up and deliver him to the shores of Nineveh. (That's an interesting mental picture: a fish on a mission from God!) There the Lord repeated His command to the prophet: "Arise, go to Nineveh, that great city, and preach to it the message that I tell you" (Jonah 3:2).

Jonah got up and started walking toward the city, saying to himself, I don't want to go. I really don't want to do this. Still, he kept walking toward Nineveh. When he arrived there, he started shouting, "God's judgment is coming! God's judgment is coming!" Throughout the city, Jonah reluctantly obeyed the Lord's command, proclaiming divine judgment wherever he went.

Suddenly all the people of Nineveh began to fast. They even made their livestock fast! The king didn't excuse anyone from fasting because he believed the word of the Lord spoken through Jonah and didn't want the city to be destroyed. And when the people fasted and repented, God relented of His plan to judge them.

Afterward, Jonah sat under a tree and complained to the Lord:

> Ah, LORD, was not this what I said when I was still in my country? Therefore I fled previously to Tarshish; for I know that You are a gracious and merciful God, slow to anger and abundant in lovingkindness, One who relents from doing harm. Therefore now, O LORD, please take my life from me, for it is better for me to die than to live! (Jonah 4:2–3)

Jonah was saying, "Oh, God, You made me a liar! I did what You told me to do. I walked around the streets of Nineveh, saying, 'Judgment is coming! Judgment is coming!' So the people repented, and You forgave them—and now I look like a liar! I knew that was what You were going to do! That's why I didn't want to go! I knew if they cried out for mercy, You would turn from Your anger, even though they deserved the judgment You had planned for them. Oh, God, why did You make me a liar? As far as I'm concerned, You may as well kill me right now because it's better for me to die than to live!"

That's why Jonah ran away: he knew that God is a loyal, covenant-keeping God. Jonah knew God was going to have mercy on the people of Nineveh, and he was more concerned about not being made to look like a liar than he was for the fate of the 120,000 people of Nineveh!

OUR COVENANT-KEEPING GOD

No matter where you look in the Bible, you find scriptures proving that God is a gracious God. He is filled with loyalty, lovingkindness, and tender mercies unto all generations.

For instance, 2 Chronicles 6 tells of the dedication of Solomon's temple. After the priests and singers fell under the power of God's presence, Solomon raised his hands before the people and prayed this prayer: "LORD God of Israel, there is no God in heaven or on earth like You, who keep Your covenant and mercy [showing acts of lovingkindness] with Your servants who walk before You with all their hearts" (2 Chron. 6:14).

Within that temple—within the very Holy of Holies—was the mercy seat of God. The Hebrew term for "mercy seat" simply meant a lid, with the implied meaning "to cover the sacred Ark" (*Strong's Exhaustive Concordance*). So throughout the Scriptures when people cried out for God's mercy, they were crying out to be covered by God's protecting hand. They were boldly claiming their right to be saved because God had made a covenant with them.

That's exactly what you need to do. You need to be bold regarding your covenant with your covenant-keeping God. Just follow David's bold request of the Lord in Psalm 40:10–11:

> I have not hidden Your righteousness within my heart;
> I have declared Your faithfulness and Your salvation;
> I have not concealed Your lovingkindness and Your truth
> From the great assembly.
> Do not withhold Your tender mercies from me, O LORD;

> Let Your lovingkindness and Your truth continually
> preserve me.

David was also bold in Psalm 51 to claim his covenant right to receive God's forgiveness for committing adultery with Bathsheba:

> Have mercy upon me, O God,
> According to Your lovingkindness;
> According to the multitude of Your tender mercies,
> Blot out my transgressions. (v. 1)

David was saying, "According to Your covenant, cover me, God. According to who You are—Your integrity, Your lovingkindness— please blot out my transgressions. I need to be covered, so I'm coming to You to ask You to cover me." And David held on to his close fellowship with God, although he suffered consequences according to the inevitable law of sowing and reaping.

Review these scriptures that speak of God's absolute loyalty born of covenant love:

> My covenant will I not break,
> Nor alter the word that has gone out of My lips. (Ps. 89:34)

> He has given food to those who fear Him;
> He will ever be mindful of His covenant. (Ps. 111:5)

> I am watching over My word to perform it. (Jer. 1:12 NASB)

God watches over His Word, eager to perform every covenant promise in response to your cry of faith. God keeps covenant; He doesn't break it. In fact, He promises to ever be mindful of His promise to perform that covenant on your behalf!

Psalm 103 explains some of the ways God performs His covenant for you:

> Bless the LORD, O my soul;
> And all that is within me, bless His holy name!
> Bless the LORD, O my soul,
> And forget not all His benefits:
> Who forgives all your iniquities,
> Who heals all your diseases,
> Who redeems your life from destruction,
> Who crowns you with lovingkindness and tender mercies.
> (vv. 1–4)

God crowns you with His lovingkindness and tender mercies. What do you do with a crown? You place it on the head of royalty. So God is saying, "I have now crowned you as king. You are a king and a priest before me. That's who you are! From this time forward, My loyal love and My faithfulness will never leave you."

Now listen to Psalm 138:2:

> I will worship toward Your holy temple,
> And praise Your name
> For Your lovingkindness and Your truth;
> For You have magnified Your word above all Your name.

God's Word is the written proclamation of God's covenant with you. That's why the Word is so important. God has made a covenant with you, and He is faithful to keep His covenant. Now it's up to you to pray as the psalmist did in Psalm 143:8: "Cause me to hear Your lovingkindness in the morning, for in You do I trust." In other words, "I want to hear Your covenant in the morning, God. I need to hear it from You."

Psalm 117 is the shortest chapter in all of God's Word, yet it also speaks of God's loyal love:

> Great is his love toward us,
>> and the faithfulness of the LORD endures forever.
> Praise the LORD. (v. 2 NIV)

God's merciful and faithful kindness is great toward you. His covenant is upon your life. He has made an agreement with you and signed it with His Son's blood.

Hebrews 13:5 (AMPLIFIED) says it all:

> He [God] Himself has said, I will not in any way fail you nor give you up nor leave you without support. [I will] not, [I will] not, [I will] not in any degree leave you helpless nor forsake nor let [you] down (relax My hold on you)! [Assuredly not!]

God will never relax His hold on you. When the pressures of life seem to come in great waves, threatening to overwhelm you and overtake your life, the covenant-keeping God will be right there at your side, speaking these words of comfort and strength:

> I will never leave you, Child, nor will I ever forsake you. I'll never turn away from you. I'll never give you up to the problems of life. I'll never turn My back on the things you're going through. I'll always be there for you, leading and guiding you, blessing and changing you into the image of My Son. I'll always be there to take the sting out of your past and to change your future into one of hope and victory. All you have to do is lean on Me, and trust in the everlasting loyalty of My covenant love.

Chapter 8

LOYALTY:
OUR LINK TO DIVINITY

A scene at the end of the new classic movie *Tombstone* often goes through my mind. Doc Holliday's life is coming to a close, everyone has left him, and some woman has taken all the piles and piles of money he accumulated through years of gambling. As Doc lies dying in the hospital, the only person who comes to see him is Wyatt Earp. Wyatt gives him a little book, and on the book cover is written, "To my friend, Doc Holliday."

Doc and Wyatt had been in a covenant friendship for many years—a friendship that had often been tested. There was the time they were caught in the crossfire of an ambush from the front and from behind. By that time, Doc was already ill and coughing continually from the tuberculosis that was eating up his body. But he stood there and fought side by side with Wyatt as the gunshots flew in every direction.

One of the men with Doc and Wyatt that day looked at Doc as he stood there coughing and shooting, shooting and coughing.

The man said to him, "Doc, what are you doing this for? You don't have to do this."

Doc turned around and replied simply, "Wyatt Earp is my friend."

The man said, "So what? I have a lot of friends."

Doc looked him straight in the eye and said, "I don't."

At the end of Doc's life, then, the only person who comes to see him in the hospital is Wyatt Earp. Doc says to him, "Wyatt, if you were ever truly my friend, or if ya ever had just the slightest of feelin' for me, leave now, leave now, please."

Wyatt looks at him one last time and says, "Thanks for always being there, Doc."

Those words were covenant words. The covenant between the two men had caused them to be steadfastly loyal to each other—even to the point of death.

LOYALTY IS DESIRED IN A MAN

In Deuteronomy 31:6, the Bible promises that your covenant-keeping God "will not leave you nor forsake you." But what does God desire of you in this covenant He has made with you through His Son? Proverbs 19:22 (AMPLIFIED) answers that question: "That which is desired in a man is loyalty and kindness [and his glory and delight are his giving]."

Understand this: what God desires in our lives is our loyalty and our kindness. And He isn't alone in that desire. That's also what other people want to know about us because "that which is desired in a man is loyalty."

We all want other people to be loyal. Even if it is a quality rarely seen in us, it is what we look for most consistently in others! How loyal are people? How deep is their loyalty in their relationships? How faithful is their faithfulness? How much lovingkindness is evident?

Loyalty is something everyone desires as a quality in his life, but few people ever achieve it. The question becomes for each person: "How much am I willing to give?"

People all over the world are crying out for loyalty—a cry for someone to walk alongside, not because he has been asked to do so, not because it's demanded of him, but just because he wants to, because he longs to, because he would have it no other way. This gut-wrenching cry, when unfulfilled, will change a person's future. It will change the countenance on his face. And it will keep him chained to the memories and the disloyalties of his yesterdays—until he is finally willing to pay the price to break the back of the generational curses of his forefathers' and his own past disloyalties.

As I sat and mused over this subject one day, this thought came to me. Integrity is the foundation upon which our life's work is built. Faithfulness is our commitment to stick to something all the way to the end. But loyalty is the refreshing aroma that is produced by the mingling of integrity and faithfulness. With loyalty we perfume the lives of all those with whom we come in contact.

That's why we are drawn toward loyalty. That's why we desire loyalty more than anything else in our relationships with our spouses, our children, our friends, and our coworkers.

A LOYAL PERSON'S DELIGHT
IS HIS GIVING

Notice in Proverbs 19:22 (AMPLIFIED) that a loyal man's delight and glory are his giving. When people look at a loyal man's life, they see that he is a loving and giving person. He consistently tries to find what he can give into any relationship. He no longer regards other individuals with suspicion. He doesn't try to cash in on his relationships by always wondering, *What am I getting out of this?*

You see, giving involves more than giving finances. The truth is, giving one's money is the smallest part of giving.

It is actually very easy to give money. All you have to do is throw money at something. But if you won't give your money, I can guarantee you that you will not give yourself to other people. Giving yourself takes every part of you. It takes your emotions. It takes your commitment. It takes your time. It takes all of you.

When we give our money, we can do it and be finished with it. It's over. This explains why we as a country, when faced with multitudes of people who had grown up with wrong parenting, didn't look for a way to reparent them. Instead, we gave them money and called it welfare.

You know, I never met anyone on welfare who didn't have other problems besides a lack of money. The reason he was on welfare was not that he lacked money. The reason he was on welfare was that he needed to be reparented.

Now here we are a generation later, and the next generation has already taken over the role of leadership. So now, living on welfare is an accepted practice because we never took care of the root of the problem. So what do we do now to change the situation? We have to realize that every time we give God's love to people, we're helping to reparent America.

Yes, it's simple for a person to give money to help someone out, but it's hard for him to give of himself. What is desired in a man is not his money, but his loyalty, his faithfulness, his covenant love.

When everyone in a room is sick, no one realizes they are sick until a well person walks into the room. When the sick ones discover the only one who was well, they turn on him and accuse him of being the one who is sick. In the same way, when everyone is unfaithful, the only one who gets taken advantage of is the one who is faithful.

Did you ever hear someone say, "Every time I try to be loyal to someone, that person takes advantage of me"? Well, do you know why that is? Because almost everyone in this world is sick. Thus, when someone wants to act faithfully in a relationship, the only protection he often receives is from above.

This is the way it will be until we as Christians learn to keep covenant. We have to be willing to stand against a society that wants to break down the virtues Jesus gave us through His work of redemption. We're the ones who have to change, for God will not. He said that what is desired in a man is loyalty and kindness, and that is what He meant!

FREELY YOU HAVE RECEIVED, FREELY GIVE

Sometimes when people talk to me about the covenant they have with God, it quickly becomes obvious to me that the covenant doesn't mean anything to them. How do I know? Because they pontificate about what the Word says, and they never act upon it. That isn't scriptural. The Bible says, "Freely you have received, freely give" (Matt. 10:8).

It is good to know what the Word of God says because it is the truth. But once you have freely received, you must freely give. The truth is, the part of the covenant that everyone can see you acting on is the only part of the covenant you actually believe. Also, notice that it is what you have freely received—not what you have freely read—that you freely give. You can give only what you have received for yourself.

If the covenant you have with God means something to you, you cannot talk about that covenant and then act disloyal to Him according to your convenience. This is another false balance— another abomination to God.

I freely receive God's faithfulness and steadfast loyalty in my life. Therefore, I must be a dispenser of God's faithfulness and loyalty into your life. I must be a dispenser of His love, His forgiveness, and His lovingkindness to you. I must be a passageway for divine blessings to enter your life, not a dam that hinders the flow of the blessings. In other words, I must help you achieve; I must not help you fail or even hope you fail.

The Bible tells us that we are to rejoice with those who rejoice and to weep with those who weep (Rom. 12:15). But if the truth be known, many times we inwardly rejoice with those who weep and we weep over those who rejoice! Why? Because we're still competing with each other. We're still trying to prove something socially and economically to the world around us.

My friend, the problems in this world will be here until Jesus returns. But as long as Satan can cause us to fight with one another, we'll never be the answer to those problems. How can we be, when we're still part of the problem?

LOYALTY IS REQUIRED OF US

Many people ask the question, "Lord, what is Your will for my life?" Then based on what they think God's will is for them, they use other people for their own selfish benefit in a carnal effort to get ahead in life.

But in Micah 6:8, God tells us what His will is for us. We must fulfill these divine requirements before we can pursue any specific assignment He has called us to accomplish.

> He has shown you, O man, what is good;
> And what does the LORD require of you
> But to do justly,
> To love mercy,
> And to walk humbly with your God?

In other words, God requires of us to walk in obedience to our covenant with Him. He has shown us what He has required of us: He requires of us covenant loyalty.

In Deuteronomy 33, God describes His loyal ones: "Yes, He loves [the tribes] His people; all those consecrated to Him are in Your hand. They followed in Your steps; they [accepted Your word and] received direction from You" (v. 3 AMPLIFIED).

John 13:34–35 notes the result of walking in covenant loyalty with other believers:

> A new commandment I give to you, that you love one another; as I have loved you, that you also love one another. By this all will know that you are My disciples, if you have love for one another.

Jesus was saying, "The world will know you are Mine because you show covenant love and tender mercy for one another. You are loyal to your brother in the Lord. You are always there for him. You are someone who can be counted on."

Do you realize that the only thing Jesus told the world to look for in Christians in order to know who they were was their love for one another? There is supposed to be more love, more commitment, and more loyalty among believers than there is among any other people in the entire world.

But that just isn't the way it is within the body of Christ. One of the most split-apart, politically motivated platforms in the world is the platform of the church.

In 1 John 3:10, the apostle John made his point again: covenant love among the brethren is the way God's children are revealed to the world. He wrote, "In this the children of God and the children of the devil are manifest: Whoever does not practice righteousness is not of God, nor is he who does not love his brother."

Far be it from us not to demonstrate that we are of God! But the world will know we are of Him only when we demonstrate covenant loyalty to one another.

EXAMPLES OF MISHANDLING
COVENANT RELATIONSHIPS

Through Jesus, we have been made covenant people. We better be careful about the way we handle our covenant relationships with other people because the One who first entered into covenant with us is intolerant of the practice of covenant breaking.

For instance, in marriage a covenant is made between the husband and the wife. When only one person in that covenant relationship keeps the covenant, an imbalance develops in the marriage. With the imbalance comes a pattern of manipulation.

The wife may crave attention so much from her distant husband that she begins to do anything to try to please her husband. Meanwhile, the husband's attitude remains: "As long as you do what I want, I'll stay in covenant with you." So the wife lives in fear of rejection, and he lives in whatever way he wants to live.

Inside that home a dull silence develops over the years. There is no real communication between the two marriage partners because the covenant was never a true covenant; it was just an agreement.

I've seen marriages in which the husband has so browbeaten his wife over the years that she just sits there and smiles. He thinks she's submitting, but she isn't. She's just tired of being told how bad she is.

The other type of marriage I often see is the one in which the wife has the strong personality. She always wants her way. She wants to control everything. In this marriage, the husband starts avoiding her. He picks up a newspaper and beer and then waits for his dinner to be served on a TV tray in front of the television.

The wife wonders why her husband never wants to talk to her, but the answer is simple: every time he opens his mouth, she finds something wrong with what he says! Every time he says something, she argues with him until she gets her way. The husband finally thinks, I'm just not going to talk anymore. It's easier if I don't say a word.

A wife like that needs to take the manipulation and control to the Cross and leave them there. She needs to take her requests to the Cross as well because she made a covenant to be something different in her husband's life.

What happens in these one-sided marriage covenants? Marriages become totally dysfunctional because husbands and wives are afraid that their spouses will break the covenant if they're honest with them. Thus, there is no opportunity for anyone to ever say anything meaningful that can help change the situation.

A similar situation occurs with employer and employees. I personally find it more difficult to confront my female employees when they give me a problem than to confront my male employees. I'll tell you why; it's simple!

If a guy gives me a problem, I can say, "If you want to make a choice to act like this, then I'll wave to you as you're on your way out!" But a woman deals in ultimatums. She knows how to stay in your face until she wins you over.

Consider the difference in the way Elijah related to King Ahab and Queen Jezebel. Even though Ahab was king, Elijah told him, "Listen, it won't rain until I say so. Well, it's time to go. Adios!"

Three years later, Elijah and the 450 prophets of Baal held a contest on Mount Carmel to see whose god was mightier. After

God had demonstrated His power to everyone present, Elijah looked straight in King Ahab's eyes and said, "Ahab, listen. I hear the sound of rain. You better start running, Buddy!"

Ahab went home and told Jezebel, "You should have seen what happened on Mount Carmel! It was awesome! God's power came down and consumed the altar, even though water had been poured all over it! Even after 450 prophets of Baal cut themselves all over their bodies to convince Baal to send fire for the sacrifice, nothing happened. And then Elijah killed all 450 prophets of Baal!"

Jezebel growled, "We'll see about that! By this time tomorrow, Elijah will share the same fate as the prophets of Baal!"

What did Elijah do when he heard what Jezebel had to say? He ran. Do you know why? Because men and women have different ways of dealing with problems! (See 1 Kings 18–19:3.)

With a male, you can say, "Listen, this is the way it's going to be." But with a female, you are better off saying, "This is going to take some prayer."

Once you have entered into a marriage covenant, do all you can to stay loyal to that commitment and to maintain a platform for communication between the two of you. If you're a husband, make sure you aren't browbeating your wife with your words. Remember, you made a lifelong commitment to her. You shouldn't be browbeating her to get your way. All you should want is God's way.

And if you're a wife, don't go around deciding which way is God's way in your marriage. For instance, wives come to the altar and pray for their husbands to get saved: "Oh, God! My husband is just horrible! He really needs to get saved. God, please save my husband!"

Eventually the husband gets saved, but by then the wife is backslidden. Why? Because she didn't really want her husband to get saved; she wanted a submitted man who would let her get her way.

THE DANGER OF MISGUIDED LOYALTIES

As important as loyalty is to the heart of God, it is also important to understand that people can have misguided loyalties. Some people stay in abusive marriages way too long. Some people stay at certain jobs too long. Others stay in unhealthy friendships, even if those friendships cause them to walk away from God. The list goes on and on and on and on.

Misguided loyalties can be found in the home, in the workplace, and among friends. There are even misguided loyalties to ideas. But when a person places misguided loyalty in a relationship, the hurtful results can mar that person forever.

You may have a misguided loyalty to a preacher you heard on a tape series. Perhaps you're more loyal to that preacher than you are to your own pastor. But where is that preacher when your back is against the wall and you're getting hammered by the devil?

One of the most common misguided loyalties is a loyalty to our own opinion at the expense of our loyalty to people. You see, before the Word begins to relieve the pressures we face every day, we don't have much time to fight with anyone. But once those pressures come off, it's easy to become a spiritual "Dead Sea" instead of a clean, flowing river if all we want to do is take in the Word but never give it out.

That's how it is for many Christians. Having freely received, all they want to do is freely receive more. They sit in the peanut galleries of life and take notes on what they don't like about other people. For months they take silent potshots at people, building a case against them according to their personal opinions. Then one day, in a second's time, they spring their case on someone. It's a case that has taken them months to form, yet they want to go to court that very second,

People don't even do that in the world! The defendant who is served papers is allowed to have as much time as it takes for him to prepare his defense. But a person who only receives the Word and never gives it out to others is loyal only to his own opinion. He demands the right to blurt out his accumulated judgment without any consideration of the person he is judging.

I'm not like that. I know I've never walked a second in your shoes. I don't know what you face every day. I want to take some of life's pressures off you, not put more pressure on you by piling on my opinions about your life.

When we cherish a misguided loyalty to our own opinions, we begin to hide behind those fig leaves I was talking about before, protecting our carnal thoughts and reasonings that lie behind the leaves. Of course, we write a Bible verse on the fig leaf so we can say that whatever is hiding behind it is okay. But we're still in bondage, no matter what it looks like on the outside.

If and Because: Two Signs
of Misguided Covenants

We find an example of a misguided covenant in Jacob's life (Gen. 28:10–22). You may remember that Jacob ran away from his brother, Esau, because he had deceived their father, Isaac, into giving him the firstborn's blessing. Jacob was scared that Esau was going to kill him for what he had done.

On his way to his uncle Laban's house, Jacob fell asleep and had a dream. In the dream, Jacob saw angels ascending and descending a ladder that extended into heaven. When Jacob woke up, he called that place Bethel, meaning "The House of God." Surely God is here, Jacob thought. Then he said this: "If God will take care of me, He will be my God."

People who say, "If God will do this," or "If God will do that," don't understand what covenant is. Any statement that includes an *if* is not a true covenant; it's an agreement.

A second example of a misguided covenant in God's Word is found in Psalm 116:1–2 (TLB): "I love the Lord because he hears my prayers and answers them. Because he bends down and listens, I will pray as long as I breathe!"

The second misguided covenant says, "Because you do this, I will be loyal to you." Such statements with *because* and *if* are not true covenants.

God desires for you and me to avoid misguided, one-sided covenants, where one party says, "As long as I do what you want . . . as long as I say what you want . . . as long as I am everything you think that you want me to be, you'll be there for me—when you want to be. But you expect me to be there for you all the time. You expect some things from me you're not willing to give." As I said before, loyalty is two-sided. It causes you and the other person in the covenant to give up what is individually yours alone.

Also, you need to understand this: you can never be loyal in any arena if you keep a plan of escape in your back pocket, ready to pull it out at any time to save yourself.

Too many times that is exactly the way we relate to God in our covenant with Him. We tell everyone that we're in faith—except we're really not. We live our lives in the realm of *if God*. Another word for that is fleecing. "If God does this, then I will do this." Does that sound familiar?

Or we live in the second realm of *because God* and mistakenly call that faith. We say, "Because You have done this, Lord, I will do this." Both ways of relating to God reveal a disloyalty inside us—an unspoken intent to back out if our conditions aren't met—that we must deal with before we can move on to win His heart.

Now, as long as so much competition exists in the church world, you can get away with a lot of disloyalty. You can leave your church whenever things get difficult and join another one, and the new congregation will usually accept you with no questions asked. As long as the church isn't operating according to covenant, you can do whatever you want, and no one will say anything.

But here's the problem, my friend: if you live like that, you will not become all that God has called you to be. Every time someone finally gets to the root of the problems in your life, you'll squirm out from under the situation. Therefore, you'll keep doing the same thing over and over and over again, all the while blaming your problems on everyone else.

As long as you run, nothing will ever change in your life. The devil knows that. When he sees you run in any area of your life, he says, "That's what I've been waiting for! I have him [or her] now!" If he sees you back off just a little, he tells his demons, "All right, let's push harder. Just push a little bit harder." And if you keep on backing off, the day will come when you will turn around and run again.

My friend, covenant works only when all parties are committed. That's why loyalty is so desired in a man!

It Has to Be Real

Too many believers reduce their understanding of covenant to mere knowledge. That's why it's no big deal to them to hop around, searching for the perfect church—something they'll never find because they aren't perfect.

A lack of understanding about covenant also explains why people look for a homogeneous group that believes the same way they do. Then when anyone doesn't believe what that group believes, the person is labeled as wrong, even "out of his tree." That's the way new denominations are formed.

But remember, when everyone is sick, no one seems to be sick. The truth is, denominations often divide us; they don't bring us together. Denominations build walls; they don't break them down.

Believers can also build walls by getting "bitten with the social bug." In other words, they start calculating within themselves,

I'm going to find ways to get close to the people in the church who are the most popular, the most affluent, or the most influential with the church leaders. But God isn't interested in that kind of cheap love. That has nothing to do with covenant loyalty.

People who think like that apparently haven't had enough tribulation in their lives yet. How can I say that? Because they are just too carnal, and the Bible is clear that tribulation develops character (Rom. 5:3–4).

Covenant loyalty has to be real, friend. With all my heart, I want it to be real in my life. I don't want to give you only the words that are written on these pages. I don't want to teach three points on loyalty and then go out and only halfway follow those principles in my life. I'm a bottom-line man, so this is how I look at it: if I'm not going to be real—if I'm not going to help change the world while I live on this earth—I might as well go home to be with Jesus today!

If I'm just going to live for myself and accomplish nothing for God, life isn't worth it to me. I don't want to stay around just to think about the extra pounds I have put in places I don't want them. I don't want to grow old just to feel bad about myself because I don't look as good as I did twenty years ago. I don't want to take space on this earth if I'm not going to change it for the kingdom of God!

Don't settle for cheap love or mere knowledge about covenant. Make it real in your life by steadfastly following the Father's example of demonstrating covenant loyalty. Therein lies the path to His heart!

• Chapter 9 •

LOYALTY IS A CHOICE

How does this situation affect me? What am I going to get out of it? To make this situation work for me, someone else might have to pay for it, but that doesn't matter to me. The only thing that matters is what I want!

This is the mind-set of a person who lives in subjectivity—seeing things only from his perspective. You can see why I say that the greatest attribute of immaturity is subjectivity.

I'll never forget the day that man I mentioned earlier sat across my desk from me and said, "The only reason I ever wanted a relationship with you was that I knew what it would do for me." At that particular moment, I felt a little like Doc Holliday in the movie *Tombstone*. In a sense, I turned my guns around and placed them on the table in a gesture of peace. Then I said, "Let's just forget about that. Now we can be friends. How can I help you?"

That day will never be erased from my memory, but I can tell you this: there is no sting in that memory. The sting has never been there. I can't tell you that I understand that man, but I don't have to understand.

You see, when you go from a life of subjective thinking to a life of objective thinking—seeing things from God's perspective—it isn't important anymore to know why people treat you the way they do. This is one reason the greatest attribute of maturity is objectivity.

LOVE COVERS A MULTITUDE OF SINS

This world desperately needs more people who see things from God's perspective. Just think about the statistics on marriage I mentioned earlier. Almost half of the first-time marriages in America today are ending in divorce. The percentages are similar with Christian marriages. People just don't stick things out because they live in their own little world of subjectivity.

But love is a choice. Commitment is a choice. Loyalty is a choice. And each one of us lives with the consequences of the choices made in relationships every day.

First Peter 4:8 tells us how to make the right choice in these matters: "Above all things have fervent [red-hot] love for one another, for 'love will cover a multitude of sins.'"

A person operating in God's kind of love overlooks the faults of the loved one, continually endeavoring to see him through God's eyes. This is the foundation of covenant loyalty.

The reason many marriages don't last is that people don't obey 1 Peter 4:8. They enter marriage thinking, *Well, I know she [or he] has problems, but once we get married, I'll be able to change those things.* As a result, they spend their married lives trying to mold the spouse into the person they want him or her to be. They have based their relationship on subjectivity, and that is definitely not the right foundation for a successful marriage.

WHEN PEOPLE BECOME DISLOYAL

The problem with subjectivity is rampant within the local church as well. For instance, some people start attending a Bible-believing church because they genuinely want to learn more about God and His Word. But somewhere along the line, they become disloyal. They decide it has gotten too uncomfortable to stay in that church, so they leave to find another one.

These people may not admit it to themselves, but they are looking for a church that has a less spiritual atmosphere and that doesn't preach the Word so strongly. They want a church where there is no pressure to change, where they can relax and sit back on their past accomplishments. What they don't realize, however, is that the point at which they became disloyal is the point at which they stopped growing spiritually.

What are the signs of a person who has chosen to become disloyal? Number one, he begins to disagree all the time. "I just don't agree with that," he says.

"That's funny. Last week you did agree!"

"Well, I don't agree with it anymore!"

You can see this first sign of disloyalty when it begins to work in people, whether it's your spouse, your children, your employees, or your church members. When you're talking to that person, you realize you're not talking to the same person you have previously known. You're talking to another person who now lives inside his body—someone with an entirely different attitude that seems compelled to disagree.

Number two, a coldness sets in between the person and those with whom he is supposed to have covenant relationship. The warmth that was once there is gone.

Number three, he starts finding fault with those to whom he is supposed to be loyal. Now he has justification for his disloyalty, and he begins to retreat.

When people begin to find fault with others, they show themselves to be the ones at fault, whether they realize it or not. They prove themselves to be disloyal and reveal their lack of stick-to-itiveness.

Mankind seems to be programmed with an inner fault of disloyalty, almost like a computer can be infected with a hidden virus. People get to a certain level in their relationships with others and then start backing off, allowing loyalty to be sucked right out of those relationships. There's so little stick-to-itiveness, even in the church.

You may be thinking as you read this: *This message on loyalty is great! I know someone in my life who really needs to read this!* But do you want that person to become loyal to you when you have never yet expected of yourself that same depth of loyalty toward him?

Friend, I'm speaking to you in this book, not to anyone else. I'm speaking only to you about your life.

If you're not satisfied with where you are in life today, consider this: perhaps the reason you're not where you want to be is that you have never walked according to this level of true loyalty I've been talking about. You may have been living your life subjectively—based on what you could get out of your relationships rather than what you could give into them. If this is the case, I pray that today is the last day of subjectivity for you and the first day you choose to live according to God's perspective of covenant loyalty.

"A Doer of Loyalty"

Here's a question that is pertinent to our discussion: Just what is a saint? Throughout the New Testament, the Bible calls Christians saints. But some people have the idea that saints are individuals who lived five hundred to one thousand years ago, had birds land on their shoulders, and spouted off wonderful little divinely inspired sayings that someone else would write down for the enlightenment of future generations.

The truth is, one definition of the word saint is "a doer of loyalty." A saint possesses the quality of loyalty, and he is a doer of that loyalty to God and to others. He knows that as he is obedient unto God, he will become loyal to God's people.

Let's examine Joseph's life once more because I believe he is one of the greatest biblical examples of a doer of loyalty. Imagine what young Joseph went through after being sold by his brothers to the Ishmaelites. At that time, a slave had to stand naked on the slave block with all his possessions lying in front of him. Then the prospective buyer would examine the slave, opening his mouth to look at the condition of his teeth, checking the strength of his arms, and so forth.

Joseph went through that humiliation. As he stood naked on that slave block for all the world to see, men stared at him and poked at him as if he were an animal. But none of that changed Joseph's resolve to stay loyal to his God.

Potiphar decided to buy Joseph and take him back to his home in Egypt. At first Potiphar put Joseph out in the field. But eventually Joseph became second in command in Potiphar's house.

Why did God make everything prosper that Joseph put his hand to? Because Joseph was a man who would never break rank. The qualities of loyalty and faithfulness, demonstrated even in slavery, caused Joseph to be promoted, no matter what situation he found himself in.

Then Potiphar's wife became interested in the handsome young slave named Joseph. When she demanded that Joseph lie with her, Joseph found himself between a rock and a hard place. But as always, Joseph made the choice to be a doer of loyalty. He told Potiphar's wife, "How then can I do this great wickedness, and sin against God?" (Gen. 39:9).

LOYALTY TO GOD FIRST—
THEN LOYALTY TO OTHERS

Notice that Joseph was concerned about sinning against God. Loyalty to God in any area of life causes a person to be loyal to others.

Everyone on this earth is capable of adultery, fornication, and other perversions in the devil's arsenal. If you have the idea that you're incapable of such things, you are gravely wrong! You are very capable of it. Your flesh screams loudly against your born-again spirit. The only thing that stops you is your commitment to God.

That's why you have to stop trying to maintain a commitment with certain people in your life that goes beyond your commitment to God. This will lead only to disappointment because people will continually disappoint you. However, if you stay loyal to your commitment to God, that loyalty will make up the difference. Remember, God—not man—is the One who will deliver you.

Just recall how it turned out for Joseph. He went from the prison to the palace because of his loyalty to God.

And once Pharaoh promoted Joseph to be second in command over Egypt, Joseph didn't walk around that palace, saying, "You know what? I've been through a lot. I deserve a little fun! I'm just going to have a little fling with sin one time. Just this one time!"

Have you ever heard of anyone having a little fling with sin only one time? Never. Joseph knew that, and his high position didn't change his loyalty to God any more than his earlier humiliation did. His answer to sin was still the same: "I cannot do this to my God."

Understand something, my friend. "I cannot do this to my God" means "I cannot do it to you either," because if I'm loyal to God, then I must be loyal to you as well. My covenant loyalty to God causes me to be loyal to you. It causes me to never take you farther than the Word of God says you should go.

My loyalty to you causes me to help you become everything God wants you to be. Our loyalty to God makes us both stand before Him with His Word as the final truth in our lives. It isn't what I think, and it isn't what you think. It is only what God thinks about any given situation.

The reason people commit adultery or get involved in other forms of sin can often be traced to this one thing: their loyalty to people became greater than their loyalty to God.

I know I am capable of adultery—not because my wife isn't everything I want her to be, but just because every person is capable of committing sin. However, I also know I will never fall into the sin of adultery. I know this, not because of anything my wife will do or will not do, but because of my loyalty to God. The answer lies inside me because loyalty must come from within.

When I am in a covenant relationship with you, my loyalty demands that I will be faithful to you, no matter what—that I will do what is right even when you don't. My loyalty to our covenant has nothing to do with your loyalty. You may cause me to have to step back, but I will never be disloyal. My hand will never be raised against you. I will never knowingly hurt you in any way.

Instead of looking for ways to step out of our covenant loyalties, we must begin to look for ways to be a cool and refreshing drink of water to the people to whom we are committed. This is the life of virtue that God is calling us to live. This is how we become people after His own heart.

FOCUS ON BEING LOYAL
TO YOUR COVENANT RELATIONSHIPS

As time goes on, we often lose our close fellowship with God because we become distracted. You see, the devil's strategies are all about distraction, whereas our relationship with God is all about focus.

I'm going to focus on living my life as a faithful man. I'm not going to be distracted. For instance, I'm not going to focus on your wife; I'm going to focus on being loyal to my wife.

You know, everyone else's wife looks good when you're not married to her. But you don't know what it took to get her out of the house today! The same thing is true with everyone else's husband.

Wives compare husbands and husbands compare wives all the time. Then they go to their own spouse and say, "I just wish you were like So-and-so." Meanwhile, the spouse is thinking, *And I just wish you'd be quiet.*

I'll tell you what ends up happening in these situations. The people who are doing the comparing fall in love with an idea. They aren't in love with a person. They aren't in love with anything real. Instead, they are in love with something they can never have. And if this happens before they ever get married, they often solve the dilemma by deciding never to make that lifetime commitment.

A lot of the distraction that results from comparing one's spouse to other people's spouses could be avoided if people took better care of themselves after they got married. When two people are dating, they always see each other at their best. The woman seems to roll out of bed looking like a million dollars. The guy regularly lifts weights and keeps himself fit and trim.

But the day after the man and woman say their wedding vows, look out! Suddenly she is dealing with Brother Couch Potato, who sits around the house all the time. Meanwhile, he's wondering who that woman is, hiding under the old housecoat and electric curlers.

That's what happens with too many married couples. They let themselves go after the wedding ceremony is over.

But it should be just the opposite. Out of your loyalty to your mate, you should take care of yourself after you enter into the covenant of marriage even better than you did before. Don't let yourself have the attitude, *Well, now I've made this covenant, but I hope nothing ever goes wrong that requires me to do anything drastic.* Instead, press in and find out how to add value to that relationship.

Your sense of loyalty should compel you to look for ways to add value to your covenant relationships every chance you get. Then when the day is done, you will be able to go before God and tell Him, "Lord, to the best of my ability, I've been loyal to my covenant with You and with others today!"

David's Sense of Covenant Loyalty

This quality of covenant loyalty that we've been talking about is the very reason God chose David to replace Saul as king. In other words, God chose David because he was a loyal man, first to God and then to other people in his life. David's commitment to God always came before the commitments he made to man.

Now, we all know that David didn't attain his reputation of being a man of covenant loyalty because he was perfect. We could pick David's life apart in fifteen seconds. We know he committed adultery with Bathsheba. We know he disobeyed

God in conducting a census of the Israelites. We all know that. Nevertheless, God said about David: "I have chosen David because he is a man after My own heart."

David's lifelong loyalty to God and to others caused the men who served David to feel a deep sense of loyalty toward him as well. We see that loyalty in action in the account I mentioned earlier about David's three mighty men and the well of Bethlehem:

> Three of the thirty chief men went down to the rock to David, into the cave of Adullam; and the army of the Philistines encamped in the Valley of Rephaim. David was then in the stronghold, and the garrison of the Philistines was then in Bethlehem. And David said with longing, "Oh, that someone would give me a drink of water from the well of Bethlehem, which is by the gate!" So the three broke through the camp of the Philistines, drew water from the well of Bethlehem that was by the gate, and took it and brought it to David. Nevertheless David would not drink it, but poured it out to the LORD. And he said, "Far be it from me, O my God, that I should do this! Shall I drink the blood of these men who have put their lives in jeopardy? For at the risk of their lives they brought it." Therefore he would not drink it. These things were done by the three mighty men. (1 Chron. 11:15–19)

David was sitting in the Cave of Adullam as the Philistines were encamped near his hometown of Bethlehem. While he sat there, David mused, "Oh, that someone would give me a drink of water from the well of Bethlehem, which is by the gate!" (v. 17).

Three of David's mighty men heard David's request before the Lord and acted on it. They broke through the Philistine lines, crept down to the well at Bethlehem, and filled a canteen with water. Then they broke through enemy lines once again, returned to David in the Cave of Adullam, and handed him that precious canteen. They had risked their lives for that water out of their deep sense of loyalty to him.

You see, loyalty makes people willing to risk everything they are for those with whom they are in covenant. Loyalty also transcends the differences that society says people have between them.

The day must come when our loyalty to each other is more important than the differences between us. The day must come when you love me more than you love what the world says and I love you more than the things that people think should separate us from each other.

However, any wall that is ever broken down between us must be broken down from within. It can never be broken down from the outside. Anything that is ever made right between us must first be made right within ourselves.

When can that "breaking down the walls" process begin? As soon as we know our loyalty to each other is true and real. This is the knowledge that makes the difference inside us.

COVENANT LOYALTY IN THE BIBLE

Loyalty doesn't have to be formed over a long period of time. It can be built very quickly if God is the Source of the relationship.

For example, take the case of Ittai (2 Sam. 15:19–21). Ittai had just come to David the day before Absalom pushed his father out of the palace. As David was leaving, Ittai said, "I want to go with you."

David asked, "Ittai, what are you doing? You've just come to me yesterday."

Ittai replied, "As the Lord lives and as my king lives, I will never leave you." Ittai might have been a newcomer in David's court, but he revealed the kind of steadfast and loyal heart that his king was desperately longing for at that time.

Then in 1 Samuel 18:1–4, David made a covenant with Saul's son, Jonathan. Apart from David's relationship with God, this covenant relationship was the one David cherished most.

> When he had finished speaking to Saul, the soul of Jonathan was knit to the soul of David, and Jonathan loved him as his own soul. Saul took him that day, and would not let him go home to his father's house anymore. Then Jonathan and David made a covenant, because he loved him as his own soul. And Jonathan took off the robe that was on him and gave it to David, with his armor, even to his sword and his bow and his belt.

In his covenant with David, Jonathan gave his friend his robe, his armor, his sword—even his right to the throne of Israel. Everything that made Jonathan who he was, he gave to David. In return, Jonathan said to David:

You shall not only show me the kindness of the LORD while I still live, that I may not die; but you shall not cut off your kindness from my house forever, no, not when the LORD has cut off every one of the enemies of David from the face of the earth. (1 Sam. 20:14–15)

We never really see David's commitment to Jonathan demonstrated until he sang his song of mourning after Jonathan died. At that time, Saul had fallen upon his own sword, and Jonathan had been killed in battle. In David's grief, he spoke about something that only he knew in his heart:

Saul and Jonathan were lovely and pleasant in their lives, and in their death they were not divided: they were swifter than eagles, they were stronger than lions. Ye daughters of Israel, weep over Saul, who clothed you in scarlet, with other delights, who put on ornaments of gold upon your apparel. How are the mighty fallen in the midst of the battle! O Jonathan, thou wast slain in thine high places. I am distressed for thee, my brother Jonathan: very pleasant hast thou been unto me: thy love to me was wonderful, passing the love of women. How are the mighty fallen, and the weapons of war perished! (2 Sam. 1:23–27 KJV)

In David's song, he said something about loyalty that you usually never hear. He said that the love of his covenant brother, Jonathan, was deeper than the love a woman could give him.

You see, the love that David and Jonathan had shown toward each other was a love that was born inside them. It was a commitment they had made in their hearts that transcended generations, for it was not only to each other, but to their descendants as well. In one sense, it was a covenant commitment that transcended even the commitment of marriage.

This covenant between David and Jonathan reveals another characteristic about loyalty: the strength of true loyalty causes it to extend from generation to generation.

As we saw earlier, David demonstrated his loyalty to Jonathan by looking for those of Saul's household to whom he could show kindness (2 Sam. 9:1–7). A servant of Saul told him that Jonathan had a son who was lame in his feet, a man named Mephibosheth. When Mephibosheth was brought before the king, David restored to him everything that belonged to Saul. And from that time on for the rest of his life, Mephibosheth daily ate at David's table.

Covenant loyalty goes far beyond just you and another person. It extends throughout generations.

The kind of loyalty David exhibited in his life can be built into your heart as well. Just draw close to the Father's heart, and allow the Holy Spirit to work on your character until it rises to the level of what Jesus has done for you!

Elisha's Covenant Loyalty to Elijah

The books of 1 and 2 Kings give us another example of a strong covenant relationship. I'm talking about the relationship between the prophet Elijah and his apprentice, Elisha. The story of their relationship begins in 1 Kings 19:19, when Elijah threw his mantle over Elisha as the younger man was plowing his fields with twelve yoke of oxen.

Can you imagine the strength of a man who can actually plow a field with twenty-four oxen? What kind of strength would a man have to possess in order to stand behind those twenty-four huge animals and keep that plow straight while they pulled it? The young man must have been massive!

Anyway, when Elijah walked up to Elisha that day and threw his mantle over Elisha, he was indicating that God wanted Elisha to be his follower. But what did Elisha do? He immediately came up with an excuse for delaying what God wanted him to do (v. 20).

People are often full of excuses when God calls them to do something for Him. "Oh, yeah, Brother," they'll tell you, "I am really committed, but I have to do this first before I can obey." No, the truth is, they're not committed!

Elisha did become a very committed follower of the prophet Elijah. In fact, Elisha stayed close by Elijah's side right up to the time when Elijah was about to go home to be with the Lord.

The relationship between these two men reminds me of the Billy Graham crusade I saw on television not too long ago. An older man hobbled up to the microphone and began singing, "I'd rather have Jesus than silver or gold. I'd rather have Jesus than riches untold."

I thought, Who is this man? Then I realized it was Cliff Barrows, a man who has given his life to helping Billy Graham become the greatest evangelist who has ever lived. Cliff was doing what he had done countless times before as he stood up there on that platform and sang, "I'd rather have Jesus . . ."

That song so perfectly defines Cliff Barrows's life. He can say, "I'd rather have Jesus! I don't care about anything else but Him. I don't really care if my name is on the sign. I don't care if I'm not the boss. I don't have to try to be somebody anymore because I'd rather have Jesus than anything this world can offer me."

When that man sat down, my heart cried out, "God, I want to be like that man. I don't want to be Billy Graham [as if anyone could ever be Billy Graham!]. But by Your grace and mercy, I could be like Cliff."

Elisha was that kind of helper to the prophet Elijah for many years of ministry. Then the day came when Elijah prepared to leave this earthly life (2 Kings 2). He said to Elisha, "The Lord has told me to go down to Bethel, but you stay here."

Elisha replied, "No, Elijah. As the Lord lives and as your soul lives, I will never leave you." So down they went to Bethel.

As they drew near to Bethel, the sons of the prophets (those in the school of the prophets at Bethel that Elijah had started) saw them and called out to Elisha. They said in essence, "Hey, Elisha, the anointing is on you! God is using you. Elijah is nothing but a has-been anyway. He is going to die; he isn't going to make it! You need to think about yourself. You don't want to lose all these schools we have going. You could run all this!"

But Elisha said, "Be quiet! I don't want to hear it. I don't want to hear anything from you!"

Then Elijah turned around and said, "Elisha, the Lord has

told me to go down to Jericho, but you stay here. God will take care of you here. God will bless you here."

Again Elisha replied, "No, as the Lord lives and as your soul lives, I will never leave you!"

When the two men reached Jericho, the sons of the prophets in the school there essentially said to Elisha, "Hey, come on, Elisha! You haven't been appreciated. You haven't gotten the recognition you should get. That's just the kind of guy Elijah is. But there are people out here who will really appreciate you, Elisha. And even if they don't, you can start something on your own. We'll back you in the ministry. We're here for you, Elisha!"

Once again Elisha replied, "Be quiet! I don't want to hear what you're saying."

Then Elijah said to Elisha, "The Lord has told me that I need to go down to the Jordan, but you stay here."

Elisha protested, "No, no, no, no! As the Lord lives and as your soul lives, I will never leave you! Never!"

So Elijah asked Elisha, "What do you want? What do I have to give you? My life is now over. The Lord spoke unto me and told me that I'm leaving."

Elisha answered, "I've watched you for years now, Elijah. I've seen the way you are. You have shown me heaven. You have shown me the Father God in ways I could have never discovered myself. I want to be twice the real man of God that you've displayed before me from the moment you covered me with your mantle."

Elijah exclaimed, "Whoa! Elisha, I can't do that. You have asked something very difficult. It isn't mine to give. Do you know that this will cost you everything? Do you know that it will cost you your life? Do you want God's presence enough to live a life of insignificance?"

Elisha responded, "I just want to be like you, Elijah."

"Well, then, if you see me as I go up, you'll know that you have your request."

Suddenly a chariot of fire appeared and picked up Elijah. Elisha watched in awe as the chariot of God ascended in a whirl-wind to heaven and Elijah's mantle descended to earth.

Elisha cried out to Elijah, "My father, my father, the chariot of Israel and its horsemen!"

Notice that Elisha didn't say, "Look what I have—your mantle! Now it's my turn to take over. I'm going to be the head prophet now. I'm going to be up in front. I'm going to be somebody. Now I'm going to be recognized the way you were!"

No, Elisha didn't do that. Instead, he ripped his own clothes in two and picked up Elijah's mantle. Smiting the Jordan River with the mantle, Elisha cried, "Now where is the Lord, the God of Elijah?"

Again, notice that Elisha didn't say, "Now where is my God?" At that moment, Elisha came fully to the place where he lost his identity and picked up the identity of Elijah. You couldn't tell anymore who was who. Elisha had paid the final price.

You see, both spiritual and natural impartation come through sacrifice. Elisha had sacrificed his natural identity to become a loyal follower of Elijah and his God. In the years to come after Elijah's departure, Elisha's prophetic anointing would exceed even that of his mentor. But that accomplishment was made possible only because of Elisha's steadfast demonstration of covenant loyalty.

THE LOYALTY OF A MOABITE WOMAN

Let's look at one more example of covenant loyalty—this time in the life of a gentile woman named Ruth.

Naomi was an Israelite woman who traveled to Moab with her husband and her two sons during a time of famine. Soon after arriving in Moab, Naomi's husband died. Life became easier for Naomi when her sons married two Moabite women named Orpah and Ruth. Both were good women who treated their mother-in-law well and stood by her side. Ten years later both her sons died as well.

With all the men of her family now gone, Naomi prepared to return to her homeland of Israel. She told her daughters-in-law, "You have both been so good to me, I could never repay you. But now my sons have died. Are you willing to wait your entire lives until I have two more sons for you to marry? That doesn't make sense. Go home to your own households here in Moab and find new husbands with whom to build new families."

Through tears, Orpah kissed Naomi good-bye. Orpah wasn't the kind of woman who was thinking, *Good! I can hardly wait to get out of here anyway!* She was a young woman who loved Naomi. But instead of sticking it out with her mother-in-law, she went back to Moab and, we hope, had a good life from that time on.

But there was a difference between Orpah and Ruth, and it centered on Ruth's understanding of true loyalty. Listen to Ruth's response to her mother-in-law's plea that she return to her parents' household:

> Intreat me not to leave thee, or to return from following after thee: for whither thou goest, I will go; and where thou lodgest, I will lodge: thy people shall be my people, and thy God my God: Where thou diest, will I die, and there will I be buried: the LORD do so to me, and more also, if ought but death part thee and me. (Ruth 1:16–17 KJV)

Naomi and Ruth traveled back to Israel together. At that point, God enlightened Naomi's heart, and Naomi remembered she had a cousin named Boaz—a rich, older man who was still unmarried.

By Jewish law, Ruth was able to glean in Boaz's fields from morning until night in order to take care of Naomi. But when Boaz heard how good Ruth was to Naomi, he showed favor to Ruth by changing the rules. No longer did she have to glean the leftovers. Now she could pick up good grain that the reapers deliberately left behind for her. Meanwhile, Boaz began to observe this beautiful Moabite woman more closely.

Then Naomi remembered that Boaz could actually be their "kinsman redeemer." He could redeem the family from poverty and shame by marrying Ruth. So Naomi told her daughter-in-law in Ruth 3:1–11, "I must now get a permanent place for you so do exactly as I say."

Ruth faithfully obeyed Naomi's instructions and found favor in Boaz's eyes. He told her, "Now, my daughter, do not fear. I will do for you all that you request, for all the people of my town know that you are a virtuous woman" (Ruth 3:11).

Ruth, a Moabite woman, later became the grandmother of David—the man after God's own heart. In her previous life, this woman had been taught to sacrifice her children to the devil. Now she had become a woman redeemed and honored by God Himself.

Orpah never experienced this blessing, and the reason seems clear. Ruth's declaration of covenant loyalty revealed the difference between the two women: "Wherever you go, I will go. Wherever you lodge, I will lodge. Your people will be my people, and your God will be my God."

Has It Been Worth the Cost?

I wish more Christians understood covenant loyalty the way Ruth did. Too many do not.

For instance, as a pastor, I often conduct marriage counseling with couples. Many times after counseling the same couples over a period of ten or fifteen years, I've found that they're still making the same blunders in their marital relationship that they did when they first got married!

Each time we meet, either the husband or the wife or both spouses leave my office, saying, "Well, that's just the way I am." They walk away, refusing to take responsibility before God to change and become the kind of husband and wife God intends for them to be.

When that happens, I just want to shake those people to their foundations and ask, "Has it been worth it for you to hold on to your own selfish feelings and opinions at the expense of your marriage? Did you gain enough from doing that to compensate for the hurts you have inflicted on yourself and on your spouse? Are you satisfied now that you have allowed fifteen of your strongest years to pass without changing what needs to be changed?"

Understand something, my friend—just as loyalty always produces a rich inheritance of blessings, so disloyalty reaps a harvest of negative consequences in your life. Of course, you can't change what you have done in the past, but you can start fresh today.

It's Your Choice

Only as you begin to think in this manner can you begin to understand the heart of God. You begin to understand the commitment that God holds in His heart for you.

As I have learned more about covenant and what it means to truly be a friend, I have repented for the years of my life when I failed to live this way. I knew I needed God's forgiveness for the times I conducted my relationships according to the ways of the world and not according to the heart of God.

I know now that, unless covenant loyalty and commitment are living realities within me, I am nothing but a miserable man. Without loyalty and truth in my life, everything else loses significance.

This is true for all of us. Life becomes shallow and without meaning when all our thoughts focus on, What's in it for me? Life can be lived to its fullest only when we live true to our covenant commitments—when we are willing to give up who we are so someone else can become the person God wants him or her to be.

Before almighty God, I say this to you: Grow up. If repentance is needed to get your heart right before God, then don't hesitate—repent! Each breath brings you closer to the end of this life. Is always trying to have your own way worth the cost? What else do you have in life if you don't have the heart of the Father?

You don't have tomorrow to change what needs to be changed. You don't even have fifteen minutes from now. All you have is right now. The present moment is your time to act because if you always wait for tomorrow, tomorrow will never come for you.

This concept of covenant love is divine, out of reach to the natural man. But you are not merely a natural being; you have been infused with the very nature of God. You have been given all things pertaining to life and godliness—everything you need to walk through this life as a person of covenant loyalty before God and man.

Just how deep can your covenant with God go? How intimately can you share the thoughts and concerns of His heart? The answer lies within you, for you are the one who must choose to walk in covenant loyalty and submission to His will.

Only you can make the decision to become a person after God's own heart. Choose wisely, my friend, and place yourself in position to win the ultimate prize—the heart of God!

FOR FURTHER INFORMATION

For additional copies of this book,
for further information
regarding Robb Thompson's ministry schedule,
or for a complete listing of Robb Thompson's
books, audiotapes, and videotapes,
please write or call:

Family Harvest Church
18500 92nd Ave.
Tinley Park, IL 60477
1-877-WIN-LIFE
(1-877-946-5433)

ABOUT THE AUTHOR

For more than a decade, Robb Thompson has pastored the congregation of Family Harvest Church in Tinley Park, Illinois, reaching out to the Chicago area with a practical, easily understood message of hope. A hallmark of his exciting ministry has been his ability to teach Christians how to act on God's Word and move out in faith so they can become winners in this life. Today, Robb Thompson's teaching ministry continues to grow through books, tapes, and the ever-expanding television program, Excellence, as he ministers to people throughout the United States and around the world.